# WILD FARE & WISE WORDS

*Recipes and Writing from the Great Outdoors*

THE SOUTH CAROLINA OUTDOOR PRESS ASSOCIATON

THE HARRY R. E. HAMPTON MEMORIAL WILDLIFE FUND

*SOUTH CAROLINA WILDLIFE* MAGAZINE

EDITED BY JIM AND ANN CASADA

# WILD FARE & WISE WORDS

*Recipes and Writing from the Great Outdoors*

Copyright © 2005

South Carolina Outdoor Press Association

Harry R. E. Hampton Memorial Wildlife Fund

*South Carolina Wildlife* Magazine

P.O. Box 167

Columbia, SC 29202-0167

Cover Art © Brett Smith

ISBN 0-9766457-0-X

Library of Congress Number
2005903452

Edited, designed and manufactured by
Favorite Recipes® Press
An imprint of

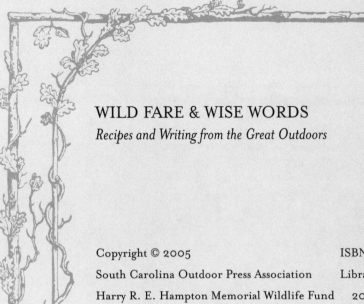
FRP™

P.O. Box 305142
Nashville, Tennessee 37230
(800) 358-0560

Book design by Brad Whitfield,
    Susan Breining

Art Direction: Steve Newman

Manufactured in USA
10,000 copies

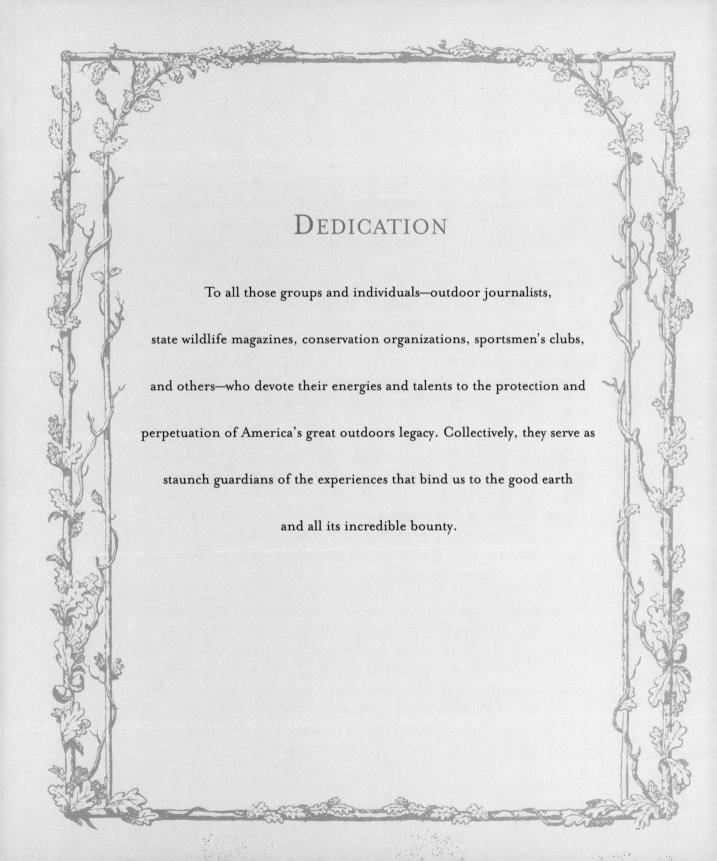

# DEDICATION

To all those groups and individuals—outdoor journalists,

state wildlife magazines, conservation organizations, sportsmen's clubs,

and others—who devote their energies and talents to the protection and

perpetuation of America's great outdoors legacy. Collectively, they serve as

staunch guardians of the experiences that bind us to the good earth

and all its incredible bounty.

# ACKNOWLEDGMENTS

Any project of this nature involves considerable input and effort from a number of folks. The separate list of contributors identifies those who have been involved in one way or another (mostly in providing recipes), but even at the risk of overlooking some individuals whose endeavors loomed particularly large in bringing this cookbook to fruition, I want to single out a number of people. First and foremost, Gail Wright has, in her typically energetic and enthusiastic fashion, been the key figure in this cookbook's production. In addition to contributing a number of recipes, she served as facilitator, cheerleader, and organizer. She also goaded me with a powerful blend of persuasiveness and amply justified impatience, all the while retaining her ever-present charm. Gail had ample backing from key cookbook committee member Pat Robertson, who with his wife, Jan, provided a number of recipes and also offered invaluable guidance while attending every planning meeting connected with the project.

Without support from the board of the Harry R. E. Hampton Memorial Wildlife Fund and input from *South Carolina Wildlife* magazine, most notably its skilled editor, Linda Renshaw, the project could not have been completed. Plaudits are certainly due to Chuck Wechsler and Larry Chesney at *Sporting Classics* magazine for their assistance with artwork. The cover art is a detail from *Early Birds*, an oil painting reproduced courtesy of Brett Smith at www.brettsmithart.com. The drawings are reproduced courtesy of Dan Metz at www.danmetzart.com and *Sporting Classics*.

Grateful appreciation is tendered to each of the wonderful folks, outdoor lovers one and all, who provided recipes for this cookbook. They are worthy followers in the footsteps of those sporting scribes who have gone before and whose quotations spice the pages of this work. Finally, a special debt of gratitude is due to my wife, Ann Casada. As is ever the case, she accomplished her portion of this endeavor well in advance and then waited with a mixture of patience and occasional petulance while I wrapped things up in my own plodding fashion.

*Jim Casada*

# CONTRIBUTORS

| | |
|---|---|
| Larry Chesney | Dan Dobbins |
| Susan H. Young | Jennifer Howard |
| Terry Madewell | John E. Davis |
| P. J. Perea | Paul Rackley |
| Betty N. Carroll | Dennis and Jane Chastain |
| Pat and Jan Robertson | Donald Millus |
| Gwen Smythe | Blake Goforth |
| Robert E. Wood | Sam Hiott |
| Gail Wright | Ben Moise |
| Captain Sammy Faulk | Jim and Ann Casada |
| T. J. Stallings | Karen Shelby |
| Bobbie and Vandy Waller | Bob Epstein |
| Morris Jarrett | John Sloan |
| Bennett and Etah Kirkpatrick | Dawn Dawson-House |
| Gene Smith | Robin LeRoy |
| Louise Eckenrod | Lynn Umstead |
| Jim Mize | Chuck Wechsler |
| Linda Renshaw | *Sporting Classics* magazine |
| Jim Goller | Dan Metz |
| Kevin Howard | Brett Smith |

# CONTENTS

# INTRODUCTION

"Supper was a delicious memory." Those simple yet superbly expressive words open what is arguably the best-known story ever written by an American sporting scribe. They introduce Nash Buckingham's timeless tale, "De Shootin'est Gent'man," and remind us in powerful fashion that a love of good food and appreciation of nature's rich bounty have always been integral parts of the outdoor experience. The ethical outdoorsman eats what he catches or kills, but the matter involves much more than the dictates of sound sportsmanship. Food fresh from the wild, properly prepared, offers delights you will never find in a five-star restaurant. That is doubly the case if special moments afield or astream produced the fine fare. "Putting meat on the table" is a quintessentially American concept and doing so brings a rare and especially rewarding sense of self-satisfaction.

Most of our country's greatest outdoor writers have realized as much, and in one way or another food figures prominently in the words they have left for posterity. Nowhere does this hold truer than in the Southern heartland, where closeness to nature, not to mention considerable dependency on her varied larder, has long been a way of life. Historical cases in point abound. For example, here in the Palmetto State where I make my home, one group of hunters from yesteryear changed the entire course of our nation's history. These were the "Overmountain Boys," staunch frontiersmen from the remote reaches of the Blacks, Unakas, and Blue Ridge along that ancient spine of time, the Appalachian Mountains.

Trained from youth as sharpshooters, these masters of woodscraft could slip through the woods like wraiths and "barked" squirrels (shooting into the bark of the tree just beneath the bushytail in order to leave the meat undamaged and facilitate retrieval of the lead bullet for recasting) as a matter of course.

At the battle of Kings Mountain, a pivotal point in the American Revolution, British redcoats and the Hessian mercenaries they had hired learned a telling lesson from backwoods squirrel hunters. Similarly, another squirrel hunter, Sergeant Alvin York, became America's most decorated soldier. On a more personal level, the finest woodsman it has ever been my privilege to know was a man from my boyhood highland homeland in North Carolina, who saw three tours of duty as a sniper in Vietnam. All of these men, along with countless others, served our country in admirable fashion because they had long been students in the school of the outdoors.

But enough of history and how the outdoors figures into our American way of life. The subject at hand is food, and in the pages that follow, thanks to a whole lot of folks who make their living communicating about the outdoor experience or who care deeply about the natural world, you will encounter scores of recipes opening doors to culinary experiences at their finest. There's probably no better way to get truly first-rate insight on how to prepare fish, game, and other foods from nature than from those whose lives revolve around closeness with the good earth. When you take their best or favorite recipes, which is precisely what this cookbook offers, you have something truly special.

One of the finest food-connected advertising slogans I've ever encountered adorned jars of a popular brand of cane syrup, Dixie Dew, which was a standard on our family table when I was a boy. Printed on the label affixed to the quart jars were these words: "Covers Dixie like the dew and gives a biscuit a college education." Rest assured that the recipes you find here represent a college education, nay, a graduate degree, when it comes to ways to prepare fish, fowl, game, and myriad accompaniments in the form of wild fruits and vegetables. My grandfather loved to describe these side dishes as "fixin's."

Another of Grandpa Joe's favorite "sayings," used when he offered richly deserved praise for one of Grandma Minnie's delectable meals, was "that's good enough to bring tears of joy to a country boy's eyes." Nash Buckingham likely felt this way when he wrote "De Shootin'est Gent'man," which is really a tale dealing with the extraordinary wingshooting ability of a gentleman by the name of Harold Money. Still, here, as in countless other cases, food memories set the stage in appropriate fashion. Sprinkled throughout these pages you will find food quotations from great sporting writers, and the remainder of Buckingham's opening paragraph is a good place to begin:

*In the matter of a certain goose stew, Aunt Molly had fairly outdone herself. And we, in turn, had jolly well done her out of practically all the goose. It may not come amiss to explain frankly and aboveboard the entire transaction with reference to said goose. Its breast had been deftly detached, lightly grilled and sliced into ordinary "mouth-size" portions. The remainder of the dismembered bird, back, limbs and all parts of the first part thereunto pertaining were put into an iron pot. Keeping company with the martyred fowl, in due proportion of culinary wizardry, were sundry bell peppers, two cans of mock turtle soup, diced roast pork, scrambled ham rinds, peas, potatoes, some corn and dried garden okra, shredded onions and pretty much anything and everything that wasn't tied down or that Molly had lying loose around her kitchen. This stew, served right royally, and attended by outriders of "cracklin' bread," was flanked by a man-at-arms in the form of a saucily flavored brown gravy. I recall a dish of broiled teal and some country puddin' with ginger pour-over, but merely mention these in passing.*

9

If those words don't conjure up thoughts of sitting down to a hunter's feast, maybe you'd just as well stick to sprouts and tofu. Similarly, if you don't know what cracklin' bread is, yours has been a life of deprivation, issues of cholesterol notwithstanding.  For the uninitiated, cracklin' bread is corn bread liberally laced with cracklings, which are the tidbits left after the rendering of lard.

Hopefully, in the material that follows, you will find plenty of reasons to celebrate success in the quest, in much the same fashion as Nash Buckingham, Robert Ruark, Harry Hampton, Archibald Rutledge, and others who have chronicled the world of the outdoors with such grace. Those of us who have contributed our favorite recipes for this cookbook can't provide the basic raw materials—venison, a brace of ducks, a stringer of fish—for their preparation. However, once you've known the joys of getting them, the road map for their preparation lies before you.

This book is arranged in simple, straightforward fashion, with eight chapters covering all aspects of the feasts and flavors available in the wonderful world of the outdoors. Some contain appreciably more recipes than others. For example, you will find dozens of ways to prepare venison. After all, a deer is a big animal providing many pounds of meat, and to offer nothing more than a couple of backstrap recipes, along with a few more using burger, would do this tasty, nutritious, and incredibly abundant game animal an injustice.

Along with the seven chapters on fish and game, there is one dealing with wild fruits, berries, and vegetables, together with a few other side dishes.

Something as simple as a family berry picking expedition can bring meaningful rewards in the form of cobblers, jams, and jellies, and Euell Gibbons was definitely onto something when, years ago, he wrote the book *Stalking the Wild Asparagus*. From persimmons to purslane, from ramps to wild raspberries, nature has all sorts of delights demanding nothing more than a bit of effort to gather and prepare them.

Join those of us who put this cookbook together, folks for whom wild fare is a part of daily life, in what we trust will be a culinary excursion into realms of pure pleasure. You'll find a little bit of everything, from the simplest of dishes to those requiring considerable effort in preparation (but worth every bit of it). Today fish and game, along with other wild fare, may no longer be essential parts of our daily diet. Yet the pervasive allure of hunting and fishing remains deeply rooted, defining elements of our unique national character. So does the appeal of consuming what these pursuits produce. All that remains is to wish you, the reader, sportsman, and outdoors lover an enthusiastic bon appétit!

*Jim Casada*

WILD FARE &
WISE WORDS

# SEAFOOD &
# SHELLFISH

# SEAFOOD & SHELLFISH

Most anywhere the sea touches the land in the South, those who know what to seek can find middens attesting to the presence of humans long before recorded history. They appreciated and utilized the bounty of the sea, gathering shellfish at low tide, as well as catching or netting shallow water fish. It was comforting to know that a reliable source of food was always readily available.

Such remains the case, although today we have to pay due heed to concerns such as pollution and overfishing. Still, there's no denying the almost inexpressible food delights yielded by the sea. Boiled shrimp or roast oysters, with melted butter ready at hand, offer a feast fit for the gods. Delicate flounder fillets, or the heartier but nonetheless delicious taste of a bluefish or mackerel, bring pure delight. Maybe your preferences run to a proper Low Country boil, with shrimp, crabs, link sausage, onions, corn, and potatoes all mixed and married in a wonderful blend of flavors and aromas. Nor should a bowl of rich, thick clam chowder, and the way in which it fills the inner man and satisfies the soul, be overlooked.

Some, of course, would argue that the simplest of saltwater fare— fish cooked over an open fire on the beach or oysters steamed over coals dampened with wet tow sacks—is the most satisfying. Pick your choice. Whatever your particular persuasion, rest assured that this chapter provides a solid sampling of saltwater delicacies and all they bring to the sportsman's table.

# BROILED BLUES

4 skinless bluefish fillets (from a 2- to 3-pound fish)
French salad dressing for coating

Juice of 1 lemon
Paprika to taste
Slices of lemon rind

Trim the bloodline of the fillets. Coat the fillets with the salad dressing and place in a broiler pan. Sprinkle half the lemon juice and paprika over the fillets. Broil 12 inches from the heat source for 5 minutes. Turn the fillets and sprinkle with the remaining lemon juice and paprika. Garnish with slices of lemon rind and broil for 5 to 7 minutes longer or until the fish flakes easily. *Makes 4 servings.*

*Bluefish meat goes soft quickly; use fresh bluefish only. Bluefish must be bled as soon as they are caught. Simply make a cut in the throat of your blue and place it headfirst in a bucket for about twenty minutes. Be sure to ice the fish well after bleeding.*

# BAKED AMERICAN ROE SHAD

1 (6- to 8-pound) roe shad
1/2 cup vinegar

1 pound smoked bacon
Salt and pepper

Skin and clean the fish, being careful to remove the roe sacks without puncturing them. Place the roe sacks in a covered dish and refrigerate. Remove the head if desired. Cover the bottom of a large saucepan with cheesecloth and place the fish over the cheesecloth. Pour the vinegar and water to cover over the fish. Bring to a boil and simmer for 2 to 3 minutes. Remove the fish from the saucepan using the cheesecloth and place in a baking dish. Layer the bacon over the fish. Season with salt and pepper. Bake, covered, at 250 degrees for 5 1/2 hours. Insert the roe sacks into the cavity of the fish. Bake, uncovered, for 30 minutes longer or until the bacon is crisp and the roe sacks are heated through. Serve immediately. *Makes 6 to 8 servings.*

# STUFFED WINTER TROUT

1 (3- to 6-pound) winter trout
   or spotted sea trout, scaled,
   cleaned and head removed
Salt and pepper
1 (14-ounce) can chicken broth

1/2 cup (1 stick) butter
1 package instant stuffing mix
4 to 8 ounces scallops, cooked
4 to 8 ounces baby carrots,
   blanched

Rinse the fish in cold salted water and pat the cavity dry. Season lightly with salt and pepper. Bring the chicken broth to a boil in a medium saucepan. Add the butter and stuffing mix and mix well. Fold in the scallops and carrots. Fill the cavity with the stuffing mixture. Seal tightly in foil. Grill the fish, seam side down, over medium-high heat for 10 to 15 minutes. Turn the fish and grill until cooked through. *Makes 2 to 6 servings.*

*This dish makes excellent leftovers. Both striped bass and bluefish work well in this recipe.*

# STRIPER PARMESAN WITH SLICED TOMATO

2 pounds striped bass fillets, cut
   into individual servings
1 cup low-fat sour cream
1/2 cup grated Parmesan cheese
2 tablespoons finely chopped
   Vidalia onion

1 tablespoon lemon juice
1/8 teaspoon hot pepper sauce
Paprika
1 tomato, thinly sliced
Fresh parsley

Preheat the oven to 350 degrees. Arrange the fillets in a greased baking dish. Mix the sour cream, 1/4 cup of the cheese, onion, lemon juice and hot pepper sauce in a medium bowl. Spread over the fish. Sprinkle with paprika. Bake until the fish flakes easily. Layer the tomato over the fish and sprinkle with the remaining 1/4 cup cheese. Broil until the cheese is light brown. Garnish with parsley. *Makes 4 to 6 servings.*

*Any flaky white fish works well in this recipe, including flounder, whiting, dolphin, or wahoo.*

# FISH PIZZAIOLA

1¹/₂ pounds grouper, dolphin, kingfish or wahoo, skin removed
1 (16-ounce) jar marinara sauce
2 tablespoons chopped fresh parsley
¹/₂ teaspoon basil
¹/₄ teaspoon oregano
Pinch of pepper
Mushrooms (optional)
4 ounces mozzarella cheese, shredded or sliced

Cut the fish into ¹/₂-inch-thick individual servings. Arrange the fish in a 9x13-inch baking pan. Spread the marinara sauce evenly over the fish. Sprinkle with the parsley, basil, oregano and pepper. Top with mushrooms and the cheese. Bake at 350 degrees for 20 to 25 minutes or until the fish flakes easily. *Makes 4 to 6 servings.*

# BLACKENED FISH

2 (6- to 8-ounce) salmon, tuna, walleye, redfish or catfish fillets
¹/₂ cup (1 stick) butter, melted
Cajun blackened seasoning

Dip the fillets in the butter and coat with Cajun blackened seasoning. Cook in a very hot ungreased cast-iron skillet over high heat for 1 to 1¹/₂ minutes per side or until cooked through. *Makes 3 to 4 servings.*

# BACKYARD FLOUNDER ITALIANO

Olive oil
4 green, yellow or red bell
   peppers, chopped
1/2 pound portobello
   mushrooms, chopped

1 Vidalia onion, chopped
8 to 12 small flounder fillets
   with skin
Salt and pepper

Heat 1/4 inch olive oil in a large cast-iron skillet over medium heat. Sauté the bell peppers, mushrooms and onion in the oil until softened. Remove the vegetables to a plate with a slotted spoon, reserving the oil. Season the fillets with salt and pepper. Cook the fillets in the oil until light brown on both sides. Add the vegetables and cook for 1 minute longer. *Makes 4 servings.*

# BAKED FLOUNDER WITH
# PARMESAN SOUR CREAM

4 flounder fillets
1/2 cup sour cream
1/4 cup grated Parmesan cheese
1/4 teaspoon paprika
1/4 teaspoon salt

1 to 2 tablespoons Italian
   bread crumbs
2 tablespoons butter, melted
2 tablespoons grated Parmesan
   cheese

Arrange the fillets in a single layer in a lightly greased 9x13-inch baking dish. Combine the sour cream, 1/4 cup cheese, paprika and salt in a medium bowl. Spread the sour cream mixture evenly over the fillets. Layer the bread crumbs and butter over the fillets. Sprinkle 2 tablespoons cheese over the bread crumbs. Bake at 350 degrees for 25 minutes or until the fish flakes easily. *Makes 3 to 4 servings.*

*This recipe can be prepared with any variety of white fish.*

# GRILLED SALMON WITH TOMATO CREAM SAUCE

6 (1-inch-thick) salmon steaks
Celery salt
Freshly ground pepper
Melted butter
1 onion, finely chopped
2 garlic cloves, finely chopped
6 tablespoons butter
3 tomatoes, peeled, seeded
  and chopped

1/2 cup dry white wine or
  chicken broth
1 tablespoon chopped
  fresh parsley
1 cup heavy cream
2 tablespoons butter, softened
2 tablespoons all-purpose flour
Chopped fresh parsley

Season the salmon with celery salt and pepper. Grill over hot coals for 5 minutes per side or until cooked through, basting frequently with melted butter.

Sauté the onion and garlic in 6 tablespoons butter in a medium saucepan until translucent. Add the tomatoes, wine and 1 tablespoon parsley and cook until heated through. Add the cream and bring the sauce to a simmer. Combine 2 tablespoons butter with the flour. Stir until a smooth paste has formed. Add the flour mixture slowly, stirring constantly until the sauce thickens. Serve the sauce over the grilled salmon. Garnish with chopped fresh parsley. *Makes 6 servings.*

"Hunger clutched at your belly and the cookin' was easy. You gutted a
bluefish, stuck him on a stick, and let him baste himself with his own fat.
His hide cracked as he cooked, but inside he was sweet as peaches."
—Robert Ruark, *The Old Man's Boy Grows Older*

# Salmon with Mango Salsa

3 tablespoons light brown sugar
1 tablespoon honey
2 tablespoons olive oil
1/4 cup Dijon mustard
2 tablespoons soy sauce

2 tablespoons olive oil
4 (6-ounce) salmon fillets
Salt and freshly ground pepper
Mango Salsa (below)

Melt the brown sugar and honey with 2 tablespoons olive oil in a small saucepan over medium heat. Remove from the heat and whisk in the mustard, soy sauce and 2 tablespoons olive oil. Brush the fillets with the olive oil mixture and season with salt and pepper. Grill over medium heat for 10 to 12 minutes or until cooked through. Serve with Mango Salsa. *Makes 4 servings.*

# Mango Salsa

3 tablespoons finely chopped
  sweet onion
1/2 teaspoon grated lemon zest
1 tablespoon lemon juice
1 large mango, peeled and
  chopped

1/2 cup chopped seedless
  cucumber
1 tablespoon chopped fresh mint
4 chives, finely chopped
1/8 teaspoon salt

Soak the onion in ice water for 10 minutes to remove some of its sharpness. Combine with the lemon zest, lemon juice, mango, cucumber, mint, chives and salt in a medium bowl. The salsa may be refrigerated, covered, for up to 2 hours. *Makes about 13/4 cups.*

# Grilled Pepper Shark

4 (1/2-pound) shark fillets
Lemon pepper
Cayenne pepper

1 onion, sliced
Juice of 2 lemons

Season the fillets with lemon pepper and cayenne pepper. Cover a grill rack with foil and heat the coals to medium. Place the fillets on the foil and layer with the onion. Sprinkle the lemon juice over the fillets. Grill for 5 minutes per side or until cooked through. *Makes 4 servings.*

# Grilled Sheepshead

2 pounds sheepshead fillets, cut
  into individual servings
Salt
Lemon pepper

1 cup (2 sticks) butter, melted
Lemon wedges
Melted butter

Season the fillets with salt and lemon pepper. Brush with half the butter. Grill, covered, over hot coals until cooked through, basting with the remaining butter. Serve with the lemon wedges and melted butter. *Makes 4 to 6 servings.*

*This recipe also works well with fresh or saltwater striped bass and other saltwater white fish.*

# Fish Marinade

3 cups lemon juice
1 cup liquid margarine
1 cup olive oil
3 tablespoons soy sauce
2 teaspoons basil
2 teaspoons dill weed

2 teaspoons parsley
1 teaspoon oregano
1 teaspoon pepper
1 tablespoon garlic salt
8 to 10 pounds striped bass or
    other saltwater fish

Combine the lemon juice, margarine, olive oil, soy sauce, basil, dill weed, parsley, oregano, pepper and garlic salt in a large bowl. Add the fish and marinate, covered, in the refrigerator for 4 hours or longer. Grill over medium heat until the fish flakes easily. *Makes 16 to 20 servings.*

# Shrimp in Basil Butter

$1/4$ cup torn fresh basil
$1^{1/2}$ cups (3 sticks) butter,
    softened
1 teaspoon minced garlic
$1/4$ teaspoon salt
$1/8$ teaspoon pepper, or to taste

$1/4$ cup freshly grated
    Parmesan cheese
16 ounces fresh linguini or
    angel hair pasta
1 pound medium shrimp, peeled
Butter for sautéing

Combine the basil, $1^{1/2}$ cups butter, garlic, salt, pepper and cheese in a food processor and process until smooth. Refrigerate, covered, for up to 3 days. Cook the pasta using the package directions. Sauté the shrimp in butter in a large skillet for 2 to 3 minutes or until the shrimp turn pink. Toss the butter mixture with the shrimp and pasta in a large bowl. Top with additional Parmesan cheese if desired. *Makes 4 servings.*

# Pickled Shrimp and Mushrooms

3 pounds peeled deveined
  cooked shrimp
2 (4-ounce) jars button
  mushrooms
2 small red onions, thinly sliced
2 cups white vinegar
1 cup ketchup

1 cup olive oil
1/4 cup sugar
1/4 cup Worcestershire sauce
2 teaspoons garlic salt
2 teaspoons dry mustard
1/2 teaspoon oregano
1 teaspoon hot sauce

Layer the shrimp, mushrooms and onions in a large bowl. Combine the vinegar, ketchup, olive oil, sugar, Worcestershire sauce, garlic salt, mustard, oregano and hot sauce in a blender container and process until mixed. Pour the vinegar mixture over the shrimp mixture and marinate, covered, in the refrigerator for 12 to 24 hours. *Makes 12 servings.*

# Pickled Shrimp with Capers

5 pounds (36- to 40-count)
  unpeeled shrimp
2 garlic cloves, minced
2 red onions, thinly sliced
1 cup olive oil
4 cups red wine vinegar

2 cups red wine
1 tablespoon salt
1 tablespoon sugar
1 tablespoon cayenne pepper
1 (3-ounce) jar capers

Bring a large pot of water to a boil. Add the shrimp and cook for 2 1/2 minutes. Drain the shrimp and soak in an ice water bath to cool. Peel the shrimp. Combine the garlic, onions, olive oil, vinegar, wine, salt, sugar, cayenne pepper and capers in a large bowl. Add the shrimp and stir to combine. Refrigerate, covered, for 24 to 48 hours, stirring frequently. *Makes 12 servings.*

# Low Country Shrimp and Grits

4 cups (or more) chicken stock
Salt
2 cups stone-ground yellow grits
1/2 cup half-and-half
1/4 cup (1/2 stick) butter
3 tablespoons finely chopped
  yellow onion
3 tablespoons finely chopped
  red bell pepper
2 ounces chopped country-
  cured ham

2 ounces chopped andouille
  smoked sausage
1 pound peeled medium shrimp
8 sea scallops
1/3 cup light madeira
1/2 cup chopped fresh cilantro
1/2 cup half-and-half
1/4 cup chopped chives

Bring 4 cups chicken stock and salt to a boil in a large pot. Add the grits. Simmer, covered, for 30 minutes, stirring occasionally. Add 1/2 cup half-and-half and stir to combine. If the grits seem too thick, stir in additional chicken stock until the desired consistency is reached. Melt the butter in a large skillet over medium heat. Sauté the onion, bell pepper, ham and sausage in the butter until the onion is translucent. Add the shrimp and scallops and cook for 1 minute longer. Add the wine and cilantro, stirring and scraping up any burned bits. Cook for 3 minutes longer. Add 1/2 cup half-and-half and cook until reduced by 1/3. Serve the shrimp and scallops over the grits and spoon the gravy over the top. Garnish with the chives. *Makes 6 servings.*

*This traditional dish is served for breakfast, lunch, or dinner in coastal South Carolina.*

# SHRIMP GRAVY

1 cup olive oil
2 large sweet onions, chopped
1/2 cup all-purpose flour
4 cups milk
1/4 cup finely chopped
  fresh parsley
2 pounds deveined peeled shrimp
Salt and pepper

Heat the olive oil in a Dutch oven over medium heat. Sauté the onions in the oil until translucent. Add the flour and stir until well blended. Whisk in 2 cups of the milk. Stir until the mixture begins to thicken. Add the remaining 2 cups milk and stir until the mixture thickens. Add the parsley and shrimp. Simmer for 5 minutes or until the shrimp turn pink. Season with salt and pepper. Serve over grits, rice, pasta or biscuits. *Makes 6 servings.*

# SHRIMP–CRAB CASSEROLE

2 pounds fresh crab meat
1 pound shrimp, cooked, peeled
  and cut into small pieces
1 cup chopped celery
1 onion, chopped
1 cup mayonnaise
1 tablespoon prepared mustard
Paprika
Salt and pepper to taste
Bread slices
Grated Swiss cheese
Grated Cheddar cheese
1 cup milk
Dash of white wine
  Worcestershire sauce
3 eggs, beaten

Combine the crab meat, shrimp, celery, onion, mayonnaise, mustard, paprika, salt and pepper in a large bowl. Trim the crusts from the bread slices and layer in a greased baking dish. Spoon the crab meat mixture over the bread. Sprinkle with Swiss cheese and Cheddar cheese. Combine the milk, Worcestershire sauce and eggs in a medium bowl. Pour the egg mixture over the layers. Bake at 325 degrees for 35 to 45 minutes or until bubbly. *Makes 6 to 8 servings.*

*The crab meat mixture makes a delicious salad.*

# RICE COOKER SHRIMP

2 pounds small shrimp, peeled
1/4 cup chopped bell pepper
1/2 cup chopped celery
1 white onion, chopped
1/2 cup (1 stick) butter, melted

1 tablespoon Cajun seasoning
1 teaspoon soy sauce
2 cups long grain rice
1 (14-ounce) can chicken broth

Combine the shrimp, bell pepper, celery, onion, butter, Cajun seasoning, soy sauce, rice and chicken broth in a 6-cup rice cooker. Cook using manufacturer's instructions. Let stand for 10 minutes after cooking is complete. *Makes 8 to 10 servings.*

# FRIED SHRIMP

1 1/2 pounds fresh shrimp, peeled
and deveined
2 cups milk
1 cup self-rising flour

1 teaspoon salt
1/4 teaspoon pepper
1/4 cup vegetable oil

Combine the shrimp and milk in a large bowl. Refrigerate, covered, for 1 to 12 hours. Combine the flour, salt and pepper in a sealable plastic bag and shake to mix. Drain the shrimp, discarding the milk. Place the shrimp in the bag in batches of about 6 each. Toss until well coated. Heat the oil to 350 degrees in an electric skillet. Cook the shrimp in the oil for about 1 1/2 to 2 minutes per side or until golden brown. Drain on paper towels. Serve immediately. *Makes 4 servings.*

# SHRIMP SALAD

1 pound cooked peeled shrimp,
  finely chopped
2 hard-boiled eggs, chopped
1/2 cup chopped celery
2 tablespoons chopped
  sweet pickles
1/2 cup mayonnaise

1 tablespoon lemon juice
1/4 teaspoon garlic salt
1/2 teaspoon dry mustard or
  Dijon mustard
1/4 teaspoon paprika
1/8 teaspoon black pepper or
  to taste

Combine the shrimp, eggs, celery, pickles, mayonnaise, lemon juice, garlic salt, mustard, paprika and pepper in a large bowl. Serve over lettuce leaves or as a filling for sandwiches. *Makes 3 to 4 servings.*

# SHRIMP CHOWDER

1/2 large onion, finely chopped
1/4 cup (1/2 stick) butter
2 large potatoes, peeled and
  chopped
1 cup boiling water
3/4 teaspoon salt
Pepper to taste

8 ounces sharp Cheddar cheese,
  grated
2 cups milk
1 pound shrimp, cooked, peeled
  and chopped
Parsley

Sauté the onion in the butter in a large saucepan. Add the potatoes and water. Simmer until the potatoes are tender. Season with the salt and pepper. Add the cheese and milk and cook until the cheese melts, being careful not to bring the chowder to a boil. Add the shrimp and simmer until the shrimp are warm. Add parsley to taste. *Makes 4 servings.*

# BEAUFORT BOIL

3 pounds smoked beef sausage, cut into 1-inch lengths

1 package seafood boil seasoning

6 ears corn, shucked and cut into halves

6 to 8 blue crabs, top shells removed and cleaned (optional)

4 pounds whole shrimp

Fill a large stockpot with 2½ gallons of water and bring to a boil. Add the sausage and seasoning and boil for 10 minutes. Add the corn and boil for 10 minutes. Add the crabs and return to a boil. Add the shrimp and cook until the shrimp turn pink. Drain and serve in a large bowl or on a platter. Serve with butter and seafood sauce for dipping. *Makes 6 to 8 servings.*

# BEAUFORT STEW

Salt to taste

Seafood seasoning to taste

1 pound smoked sausage, cut into 1½-inch pieces

1 large onion, chopped (optional)

8 red potatoes, cubed

8 ears corn

2 pounds (36- to 40-count) shrimp

Fill a large stockpot half full with water and bring to a boil. Season the water with salt and seafood seasoning. Add the sausage, onion and potatoes and boil for 7 to 8 minutes. Add the corn and boil for 8 to 10 minutes. Remove the sausage, corn, onion and potatoes with a slotted spoon and set aside. Add the shrimp to the stockpot and return to a boil. Cook until the shrimp turn pink. Remove the shrimp with a slotted spoon and place in a large bowl of ice water to stop the cooking process. Combine the sausage, onion, potatoes, shrimp and corn in a large serving dish. Serve with butter and cocktail sauce. *Makes 4 servings.*

# FROGMORE STEW

1 cup Old Bay seasoning
6 ears fresh corn or
   12 frozen corncob halves
2 pounds smoked kielbasa, cut
   diagonally into 1-inch pieces

3 pounds (36- to 40-count)
   shrimp
Additional Old Bay seasoning

Bring a large stockpot of water to a boil. Add the Old Bay seasoning and corn. Boil for 4 minutes for fresh corn or for 8 minutes for frozen corn. Add the sausage and return to a boil. Boil for 3 minutes. Add the shrimp and boil for 2¹/₂ minutes. Drain well. Sprinkle generously with additional Old Bay seasoning. Serve on a large platter or pour onto newspaper spread over a tabletop. Serve with coleslaw, cocktail sauce and liquid margarine. *Makes 6 servings.*

# SEAFOOD FETTUCCINE ALFREDO

8 ounces scallops
8 ounces peeled shrimp
1 tablespoon butter
2 garlic cloves, minced
2 cups heavy cream

Dash of oregano or Greek
   seasoning
16 ounces fettuccine, cooked
   and drained
Grated Romano cheese

Sauté the scallops and shrimp in the butter in a saucepan until the scallops are white and opaque and the shrimp turn pink. Remove the scallops and shrimp with a slotted spoon. Sauté the garlic in the saucepan. Add the cream and oregano. Cook until heated through. Pour the sauce over the fettuccine in a serving bowl. Add the scallops and shrimp. Sprinkle with Romano cheese. Toss to mix. *Makes 4 servings.*

# Coquilles St. Jacques

2 cups white wine
1 tablespoon minced shallots or onions
3 pounds small or medium bay scallops
1/2 cup (1 stick) butter
1 1/4 cups all-purpose flour
1 cup heavy cream
4 egg yolks
1 cup shredded Swiss cheese
1 pound fresh mushrooms
Butter
1 cup bread crumbs

Bring the wine and shallots to a boil in a large stockpot. Add the scallops and cook for 3 minutes or until white and opaque. Remove the scallops with a slotted spoon, reserving the wine. Cook the wine over high heat until reduced to 1 cup. Melt 1/2 cup butter in a saucepan. Add the flour and cook until bubbly. Add the reserved wine and simmer for 15 minutes.

Beat the cream and egg yolks together in a small bowl. Add the egg mixture to the wine mixture. Cook for 1 minute longer. Add the cheese, stirring until melted.

Sauté the mushrooms in butter in a saucepan over high heat. Drain and add to the sauce. Add the scallops. Spoon the scallop mixture into ramekins or scallop shells. Sprinkle with the bread crumbs. Bake in a hot oven until the bread crumbs begin to brown. *Makes 6 servings.*

# Traditional Southern Oyster Roast

12 to 24 live oysters per person
Tabasco sauce

Seafood sauce
Saltines

Soak a large piece of burlap in salted water for 15 minutes. Place the oysters on the grill over high heat. Cover the oysters with the wet burlap. Cook until the oysters open, turning once after about 7 minutes. Serve hot with Tabasco sauce, seafood sauce and saltines. *Servings vary.*

*While wet burlap will hold more steam and create more succulent oysters, it is not necessary. The oysters can be roasted directly without any cover.*

# Oyster Dressing

1 (8-ounce) can oysters
1 (10-ounce) can cream of
  mushroom soup
2 eggs

1 1/2 sleeves butter crackers
1/4 cup (1/2 stick) butter,
  cut into small pieces

Drain the oysters, reserving the liquor and checking for pieces of broken shell. Combine the reserved liquor with the soup and eggs in a bowl. Place a layer of crackers over the bottom of a 9-inch square baking dish. Layer the oysters over the crackers. Spread the soup mixture evenly over the oysters. Crush the remaining crackers and sprinkle evenly over the layers. Layer the butter over the crackers. Bake, covered, at 350 degrees for 45 minutes. Remove the cover and bake for an additional 15 minutes. *Makes 4 to 6 servings.*

*Oyster Dressing is the perfect accompaniment to wild turkey, fried quail, or dove.*

# OYSTER STEW

2 (12-ounce) cans oysters
2 sweet onions, chopped
1/2 cup olive oil
1 teaspoon self-rising flour
4 cups milk

1 tablespoon dried parsley
1 teaspoon seasoned garlic salt
1/2 teaspoon pepper
Oyster crackers or saltines

Drain the oysters, checking for pieces of broken shell. Sauté the onions in the olive oil in a Dutch oven over medium-high heat. Add the flour, whisking until blended. Add the oysters and stir to combine. Stir in the milk, parsley, garlic salt and pepper. Bring to a boil and remove from the heat. Serve immediately with oyster crackers or saltines. *Makes 4 servings.*

# SALMON CHEESE BALL

1 (6-ounce) can salmon,
  drained
1/2 cup chopped onion
1/2 cup chopped green
  onions
8 ounces cream cheese

1 cup shredded sharp Cheddar
  cheese
1 cup shredded Monterey Jack
  cheese
1/2 cup dried parsley
1/2 cup finely chopped pecans

Combine the salmon, onion, green onions, cream cheese, Cheddar cheese and Monterey Jack cheese in a large bowl. Form into a ball. Combine the parsley and pecans in a large shallow dish. Roll the ball in the parsley mixture until completely covered. Serve with crackers. *Makes 5 cups.*

"The Old Man used to say, 'There ain't no such thing as
*enough* oysters—it's just that the human stomach was never
really designed to handle a decent bait of them.'"
—Robert Ruark, *The Old Man and the Boy*

# Salmon Melts

2 (7-ounce) cans salmon or
   tuna, drained
1/4 cup ranch salad dressing
1 teaspoon lemon juice
1/4 cup chopped sweet onion

4 English muffins, halved and
   toasted
4 slices Swiss or provolone
   cheese, halved diagonally

Combine the salmon, salad dressing, lemon juice and onion in a large
bowl. Place the muffin halves, cut side up, on a baking sheet. Spoon equal
portions of the salmon mixture over the muffin halves. Place a slice of the
cheese over the salmon mixture. Broil until the cheese melts. *Makes 4 servings.*

# Tuna Melts

1 (6-ounce) can tuna, drained
   and rinsed
4 ounces sharp Cheddar cheese,
   cut into cubes

1/2 cup chopped celery
Pepper to taste
1/3 cup mayonnaise or to taste
4 hamburger buns, halved

Combine the tuna, cheese, celery, pepper and mayonnaise in a bowl.
Spoon the tuna mixture over the bottom halves of the hamburger buns.
Place the top halves of the buns over the tuna mixture. Wrap the sandwiches
in foil and bake at 350 degrees for 20 minutes or until the cheese melts.
*Makes 4 servings.*

# Roman Tuna Salad

1 (6-ounce) can water-pack
    tuna, or 1 pound tuna steak,
    cooked
1 heaping tablespoon Caesar
    salad dressing
1 tablespoon drained capers
1 rib celery, finely chopped
1 tablespoon sliced black olives
1 tablespoon dried parsley
Crusty bread
Lettuce
Tomato slices

Drain and flake the canned tuna or cut the tuna steak into 1/2-inch
pieces. Combine the tuna, salad dressing, capers, celery, olives and parsley
in a large bowl. Serve on crusty bread with lettuce and tomato slices.
*Makes 3 to 4 servings.*

# Moise Island Potato Crab Cakes

2 large potatoes, baked, peeled
    and mashed
Salt
Pepper
1/2 cup chopped onion
1/2 cup chopped bell pepper
1 tablespoon cornstarch
1 egg
12 crabs, boiled and flaked
Vegetable oil for frying
Cornmeal for coating

Combine the potatoes, salt, pepper, onion and bell pepper in a large
bowl. Add the cornstarch; stir to combine. Combine the egg and crab meat
in a small bowl. Add to the potato mixture and stir to combine. Heat about
1/2 inch vegetable oil in a large skillet over medium heat. Form the potato
mixture into 3-inch patties and coat in cornmeal. Fry in the hot oil until
brown on both sides. *Makes 3 to 4 servings.*

# Valentine Chowder

2 fish bouillon cubes
5 bay leaves
1 teaspoon Old Bay seasoning
1 pound unpeeled shrimp
2 slices bacon or turkey bacon
1 large onion, chopped
1 large red bell pepper, minced
1/4 cup (1/2 stick) butter
2 heaping tablespoons
　all-purpose flour
1 (10-ounce) can chicken broth
1 cup water
4 russet potatoes, peeled and
　finely chopped

1 tablespoon Old Bay seasoning
1/2 teaspoon cayenne pepper
1/2 teaspoon ground nutmeg
1 teaspoon salt
1/2 teaspoon black pepper
4 whole dried dundicott peppers
　or Scotch bonnet peppers
1 tablespoon Worcestershire
　sauce
2 cups frozen corn
1 pound back-fin crab meat
1 cup half-and-half or
　heavy cream
1/2 cup dry sherry

Fill a medium stockpot 3/4 full with water. Add the bouillon cubes, 2 bay leaves and 1 teaspoon Old Bay seasoning and bring to a boil. Add the shrimp and cook for 2 to 3 minutes or until the shrimp turn pink. Remove the shrimp with a slotted spoon. Cool completely and peel, reserving the shells. Refrigerate the shrimp. Add the shells to the seasoned water and boil for 30 minutes. Drain and reserve the shrimp stock.

Sauté the bacon, onion and red bell pepper in the butter in a large stockpot until the onion is soft. Whisk in the flour until blended. Stir in the chicken broth and water. Bring to a boil. Add the potatoes, 3 bay leaves and the next 7 ingredients. Boil for 30 minutes or until the potatoes begin to soften. Remove half the potatoes with a slotted spoon. Mash the potatoes in a bowl with a potato masher or an immersion blender. Return the mashed potatoes to the stockpot.

Add the reserved shrimp stock to the potato mixture. Add water as needed to fill the pot 3/4 full. Stir in the corn and crab meat. Cook until the corn is heated through. Add the reserved shrimp and half-and-half. Remove and discard the bay leaves and whole peppers. Adjust the seasonings to taste. Pour the sherry over the soup just before serving. *Makes 6 servings.*

# HOT CRAB DIP

1 white onion, chopped
1/4 cup finely chopped red bell pepper
1/4 cup finely chopped celery
1 teaspoon minced garlic
1/4 teaspoon salt
1 tablespoon Cajun seasoning
1/2 cup (1 stick) butter
1 (10-ounce) can roasted garlic soup
1 (5-ounce) can evaporated milk
1 pound crab meat
1 bunch green onions, chopped

Sauté the onion, bell pepper, celery, garlic, salt and Cajun seasoning in the butter until the vegetables are soft. Add the soup and milk and bring to a boil. Add the crab meat and simmer for 10 minutes.

Stir in the green onions. Spoon the dip into a serving dish and cool for 10 minutes before serving.

Serve with chips and crackers or as a topping over broiled chicken breasts, pork chops or venison steaks. *Makes about 5 cups.*

"I feel real sorry for people who never had a chance at broiled
bluefish or mackerel when the fish is so fresh you have to kill him
before you clean him. Some say that blues and mackerel are too
fat and oily, but there are some people who don't like
snails or oysters and think carrots are just dandy."
—Robert Ruark, *The Old Man and the Boy*

WILD FARE &
WISE WORDS

# FRESHWATER
# FISH

# FRESHWATER FISH

Over a marvelously misspent life in which days afield and astream have loomed large, it has been my privilege to eat many grand meals where fish or game formed the entrée. Then, too, there have been plenty of field lunches occasioned by hunting pursuits that have their special place in memory's fond storehouse. It's little short of miraculous the way the most humble fare—a tin of sardines or Vienna sausages, a chunk of cold corn bread and a raw onion, apples or oranges, a Moon Pie accompanied by a belly washer, maybe a slice of cake or homemade cookies—becomes festive fare thanks to the setting.

But were I faced with the difficult choice of deciding on the finest of all food offerings enjoyed by the outdoorsman, I would opt for freshwater fish fried shortly after being caught. Lots of species found in freshwater have their merits. Fillets from hand-sized bluegills or crappie, dipped in cornmeal and fried to a golden brown, will tempt you to eat to total satiation. A shore lunch featuring fresh walleye, with sides of fried potatoes and onions, inevitably bids fair to leave you as full and happy as an old hound sleeping in the sunshine. Even the humble, ugly catfish, which tastes as good as it looks ugly, can put in a bid for top slot in the fish for the table sweepstakes.

Yet for all the lusciousness of these and other feasts of fish, give me four or five brook trout (or specks, as they are called by many mountain folks). Cook a few strips of bacon for the grease, give the trout corn bread overcoats, dust them with salt and pepper, and then fry the trout until golden brown. Eat with your fingers while the trout are still piping hot, maybe with a wild salad of branch lettuce and ramps sprinkled with the bacon you cooked and a bit of the leftover grease, and you have a gustatory delight beyond compare.

Whatever your personal preferences, and whether you eat fish at streamside or on the lakeshore, at a backyard fish fry, or as haute cuisine at a decorative dining table, these recipes should pique your interest and tickle your palate.

# CATFISH STEW

6 to 7 pounds catfish fillets
5 pounds potatoes
3 pounds onions, diced
1 to 1½ pounds lean hog jowl or
    side meat, diced
1 (27-ounce) can diced tomatoes
3 (14-ounce) cans stewed
    tomatoes

1 (46-ounce) can tomato
    juice
¼ cup Worcestershire sauce
Salt, black pepper and red
    pepper to taste
Hot red pepper sauce

Combine the catfish and enough water to cover in a soup pot. Bring to a boil, then simmer until the fish flakes easily. Drain and reserve the cooking liquid. Pick through the fish to remove any bones. Refrigerate the fish.

Peel potatoes (or leave peels on, if using red potatoes) and cut into ½-inch cubes. Add to the pot of fish stock.

Combine the onions with water to cover in a saucepan and bring to a boil. Cook until tender, then add to the soup pot.

Fry the jowl until crisp. Drain and add the meat to the soup pot.

Add the fish to the pot along with the diced tomatoes. Cut the stewed tomatoes into small pieces and add to the soup.

Add tomato juice as needed to prevent the mixture cooking down too much. When potatoes and onions are tender, add the Worcestershire sauce.

Taste and season with salt, peppers and hot pepper sauce. Simmer for 2 to 3 hours, stirring occasionally. *Makes about 15 servings.*

# CAJUN CATFISH SAUCE PIQUANT

1 tablespoon cayenne pepper
2 1/2 teaspoons salt
2 teaspoons black pepper
3 pounds catfish fillets, thoroughly skinned and all red meat removed
2 cups finely chopped onions
1 tablespoon vegetable oil

1 tablespoon all-purpose flour
1 1/2 cups finely chopped green bell pepper
1/2 cup finely chopped celery
1/2 cup chopped garlic
3 1/2 cups chicken stock
2 (8-ounce) cans tomato sauce
1 tablespoon lemon juice

Combine the cayenne pepper, salt and black pepper in a small bowl. Sprinkle about 2 teaspoons of the mixture over the fish and work it into the fish. Refrigerate the fish until ready to cook.

Have the onions at hand to add to the roux. Combine the oil and flour in a heavy 6-quart saucepan and mix well. Cook the mixture over high heat for 5 to 7 minutes, stirring constantly, until the mixture is medium brown. Remove from heat and stir in the onions. Return to high heat and cook for 1 minute, stirring constantly. Add the bell pepper, celery and garlic and mix well. Stir in 1 cup of the stock and the remaining pepper and salt mixture. Bring to a boil and cook for 5 minutes, stirring occasionally. Reduce heat to low and stir in the tomato sauce. Cook for 45 minutes, stirring occasionally. Add 1 cup more stock and cook for 25 minutes. Add the remaining stock and lemon juice and cook for 15 minutes, stirring constantly. Add the fish and cover the pan. Bring to a boil over high heat. Stir occasionally, carefully, so as not to break up fish pieces. Reduce heat to low; cover the pan and cook for an additional 20 minutes. Remove from heat and skim any fat from the surface. Serve immediately over rice with French bread for dipping. *Makes 10 to 15 servings.*

*This stew tastes better the second day and freezes well.*

# Catfish Pâté

1 pound catfish fillets
$1/2$ cup water
16 ounces cream cheese,
softened
1 garlic clove, minced

2 tablespoons minced onion
2 tablespoons fresh lemon juice
2 tablespoons Creole seasoning
Salt and freshly ground pepper
to taste

Poach the fish in the water in a saucepan until the fish flakes easily;
drain. Combine the fish with the cream cheese, garlic, onion, lemon juice,
Creole seasoning, salt and pepper in a food processor and process until
smooth. Spoon into a container; cover and chill for 2 hours. Serve with
pepper crackers or garlic toast. *Makes 16 servings.*

# Spicy Catfish Nuggets

2 pounds catfish, cut into
1- to $1^{1}/_{2}$-inch pieces
1 bottle buffalo-style hot wing
sauce

6 cups cornmeal
Salt and pepper to taste
2 to 3 quarts peanut oil or other
vegetable oil for deep-frying

Marinate the catfish pieces in the sauce for up to 30 minutes. Season
the cornmeal with salt and pepper to taste, bearing in mind that the
wing sauce is strongly seasoned.

Heat the oil to 375 degrees in a deep pot. Toss the catfish with the
cornmeal in a bowl or paper bag. Cook the nuggets, a few at a time,
until they float to the top and are golden brown. Drain on paper towels.
*Makes 10 to 12 servings.*

# SIMPLE CATFISH FILLETS

1 cup lemon juice
2 pounds catfish fillets

Grill seasoning

Pour the lemon juice into a bowl. Dip the fish into the juice, then sprinkle generously with seasoning. Cook on a grill pan or in an oiled skillet for 10 minutes per inch of thickness or until the fish flakes easily. *Makes 4 servings.*

# MEDITERRANEAN-STYLE CATFISH

4 catfish fillets
Salt and pepper to taste
3 tablespoons olive oil
2 garlic cloves, minced
1/2 red onion, thinly sliced
2 tablespoons balsamic or red wine vinegar
2 tablespoons lemon juice

1 cup marinated artichoke hearts, quartered
2 tablespoons chopped black olives
1 cup seeded and diced tomato or canned tomato, drained
1/2 cup crumbled feta cheese

Sprinkle the fish evenly with salt and pepper. Heat the oil in a large nonstick skillet over medium heat. Add the catfish fillets and cook for 5 minutes. Turn the fish and add the garlic and onion. Cook for an additional 5 minutes. Add the vinegar, lemon juice, artichokes, olives and tomato. Cook for 3 to 4 minutes to make a chunky sauce. Place the fish on a platter and spoon the sauce over the top. Sprinkle with the feta cheese. Serve with hearty bread and couscous. *Makes 4 servings.*

# Southern-Style Catfish Cakes with Chili-Tarragon Vinaigrette

### CHILI-TARRAGON VINAIGRETTE
$^1/_4$ cup champagne vinegar
3 tablespoons chopped fresh
 tarragon
2 garlic cloves, minced
1 teaspoon freshly ground
 black pepper
2 tablespoons minced
 jalapeño pepper
3 tablespoons fresh lime juice
6 tablespoons mayonnaise
1 tablespoon Dijon mustard
$^1/_4$ cup fresh lemon juice

### CATFISH CAKES
2 tablespoons lemon pepper
$^1/_4$ cup chopped green onions
1 cup Italian bread crumbs
1 egg
$^1/_2$ cup mayonnaise
1 teaspoon Worcestershire sauce
$1^1/_2$ pounds catfish fillets,
 minced
$^1/_2$ cup vegetable oil
Cooked pasta, for serving

For the vinaigrette, combine all the ingredients in a bowl and beat vigorously with a whisk until well blended.

For the catfish cakes, combine the lemon pepper, green onions, bread crumbs, egg, mayonnaise and Worcestershire sauce in a medium bowl and mix well. Add the catfish and mix well. Add more mayonnaise or bread crumbs to obtain a consistency that holds together without crumbling but is not wet. Form the mixture into 8 round cakes about 4 inches in diameter and 3/4 inch thick.

Heat the oil in a skillet over medium heat. Add the catfish cakes and cook on each side for about 5 minutes or until brown. Serve on a bed of pasta, drizzled with the vinaigrette. *Makes 4 servings.*

# SOUR CREAM–SMOTHERED CATFISH

4 catfish fillets
1 cup zesty Italian salad dressing
1 onion, coarsely chopped
1 green bell pepper, chopped
1 tomato, chopped

1 lemon, thinly sliced
1 (8-ounce) carton sour cream
1 teaspoon Cajun seasoning
Salt and pepper to taste
3 cups cooked rice

Pat the catfish fillets dry. Cut the fish into large chunks (about 6 pieces per fillet). Combine the fish with the dressing in a plastic bag and marinate for 30 minutes. Remove the fish and discard the marinade.

Preheat the oven to 350 degrees. Place the fish in a baking dish and cover with the onion, bell pepper, tomato and sliced lemon. Cover all with sour cream. Sprinkle with Cajun seasoning, then salt and pepper to taste.

Bake until the fish flakes easily with a fork, about 35 to 45 minutes. Serve over cooked rice with a green salad and freshly baked bread. *Makes 4 servings.*


# HONEY PECAN MOUNTAIN TROUT

2 pounds trout fillets
1/2 cup all-purpose flour
Salt and pepper to taste
1/2 cup finely ground pecans

1 egg or egg white, beaten
Butter, softened
Honey

Fillet the trout if large. Smaller fish may be split down the middle and as many bones removed as possible, leaving the skin and scales on.

Preheat a grill, broiler or grill pan. Combine the flour, salt and pepper. Spread the pecans on a clean plate or a sheet of waxed paper. Dip the fish in the flour mixture and shake off excess. Brush with the egg, then press the fish into the pecans. Dot the fish with butter and drizzle with a little honey. Grill, skin side down first, until partially cooked, then turn and cook through. *Makes 4 servings.*

# CRAB-STUFFED RAINBOW TROUT

1 tablespoon olive oil, plus additional for coating fish
1 tablespoon finely diced onion
1 tablespoon finely diced celery
2 tablespoons butter
1 cup crab meat (about 5 ounces)
1/4 cup Italian-seasoned bread crumbs
1/4 cup crushed saltine crackers
1 tablespoon lemon juice
1/4 teaspoon Old Bay seasoning
1/4 teaspoon pepper, plus additional for seasoning trout
5 or 6 wild rainbow trout, or 2 farm-raised rainbow trout,
    about 1 1/2 pounds total, cleaned and left whole
Kosher salt and pepper

Prepare a grill for direct grilling over medium heat. Heat 1 tablespoon oil in a saucepan over medium heat and sauté the onion and celery for about 2 minutes. Add the butter, crab meat, bread crumbs, cracker crumbs, lemon juice and seasonings and mix gently but thoroughly.

Spoon stuffing into the cavity of each fish. Coat the fish all over with olive oil and place in a grilling basket. Season with salt and pepper to taste. Grill the fish, turning occasionally, for about 10 minutes, or until the fish are golden and flake easily. *Makes 2 servings.*

*Trout abound in the mountain streams of North Carolina. Small to medium trout (8 to 14 inches) taste better than large ones.*

# CANNED TROUT

Trout                          Salt
Red pepper flakes              Bay leaf

Cut thoroughly cleaned fish into 2-inch chunks or pieces that will fit
into pint jars. Pack the fish into jars. Add to each jar $^1/_8$ teaspoon red
pepper flakes, $^1/_2$ teaspoon salt and $^1/_2$ bay leaf. DO NOT ADD WATER.
Put on the lids and put the jars in a pressure cooker. Cook for 90 minutes
at 10 pounds pressure. *Yield varies.*

# TROUT SOUP WITH DILL

4 trout, cleaned, heads removed
2 medium potatoes, diced
2 carrots, diced
1 (10- to 14-ounce) can
   chicken broth
2 cups water
2 green onions, chopped
1 cup milk

1 (8-ounce) package full-fat or
   reduced-fat cream cheese,
   cut into chunks
2 teaspoons dried dill
Salt and freshly ground pepper
   to taste
Fresh dill sprigs for garnish

Poach the trout in 1 inch of water in a saucepan until the fish flakes
easily. Remove the trout from the pan; remove the skin and flake the fish
from the bones. Boil the potatoes and carrots in the chicken broth and
water in a saucepan until tender. Remove the vegetables from the broth
mixture and set aside. Reduce heat to low. Add the green onions, milk,
cream cheese and dried dill, stirring and heating until the mixture is smooth
and creamy. Do not boil or the mixture may curdle. Add the cooked
potatoes and carrots. Add the flaked fish and a little more water or chicken
broth if needed. Season with salt and pepper to taste and heat through.
Garnish with fresh dill. Serve with a green salad and hot rolls.

# No-Mess Grilled Trout

Several pan-size trout
Vegetable oil
Salt

Butter
Lemon juice

The secret to this recipe is properly cleaning the trout. Cut off the head and slice open the belly to remove the innards. Holding the fish belly side up, cut directly into the backbone to split it so the fish opens up to lie flat. Do this without piercing the skin. Brush the outside skin with oil. Grill the fish, skin side down. As it heats, it will tighten and create a bowl. Salt lightly, top with a slice of butter, and squeeze a little lemon juice on each fillet. In a few minutes, the skin will be crackly and the meat will become flaky. Scoop off the grill with a spatula. *Yield varies.*

*Try substituting your favorite salsa for the lemon and butter.*

# Parmesan Bream

Bream fillets
Shredded Parmesan cheese

Salt and pepper to taste

Preheat the oven to 325 degrees. Spray a baking dish with nonstick cooking spray. Arrange fillets in a single layer and sprinkle generously with cheese. Arrange another layer of fish over the cheese, then top with more cheese. Continue layering until there are 3 or 4 layers of fish. Bake for about 40 minutes, watching closely so fish doesn't overcook. *Yield varies.*

# CRAPPIE DELIGHT

2 pounds crappie fillets
1/4 cup lemon juice
2 eggs, beaten
1/4 cup milk

1 teaspoon salt
1 cup all-purpose flour
Oil for frying
1/2 cup grated Cheddar cheese

Cut the fillets into serving-size portions and arrange in a baking dish. Pour the lemon juice over the fish and let stand for 6 to 8 minutes, turning once. Combine the eggs, milk and salt in a bowl. Roll the fillets in the flour, then dip into the egg mixture. Heat the oil in a large skillet and fry the fish until brown on 1 side, then turn. Sprinkle cheese on the cooked side—it will melt as the fish cooks. Serve immediately. *Makes 4 servings.*

# CRAPPIE CASSEROLE

1 cup (or more) cracker crumbs
1 1/2 to 2 pounds crappie fillets,
   all bones removed

Salt and pepper to taste
1 pound grated cheese
Butter or margarine

Preheat the oven to 350 degrees. Grease a 2-quart baking dish. Sprinkle with some of the cracker crumbs. Layer the fish fillets in the dish and season with salt and pepper. Cover with a generous layer of cheese and top with more cracker crumbs. Dot with butter or margarine. Repeat the layers until all fillets are used. Bake for 45 minutes or until the top crust of buttered crumbs has browned. Serve hot. *Makes 6 to 8 servings.*

# FRIED CRAPPIE

1 pound self-rising yellow
   cornmeal
1 teaspoon salt
1/4 teaspoon pepper
1 (12-ounce) can evaporated
   milk

3 eggs, slightly beaten
12 whole crappie, cleaned
1 gallon cooking oil

Combine the cornmeal, salt and pepper in a paper bag. Pour the evaporated milk and eggs into a shallow dish and mix well. Dip the fish into the milk mixture, then shake with the cornmeal mixture in the paper bag. Heat the oil to 350 degrees in a deep fryer. Cook the crappie in the hot oil until golden brown, about 4 to 6 minutes. Drain on paper towels and serve hot. *Makes 4 servings.*

# JERKED STRIPED BASS

6- to 8-ounce striped bass fillet
   per person, skinned and
   deboned, with most dark meat
   removed

Caribbean jerk marinade
1 pineapple ring per fillet

Cover the fish with marinade in a bowl and refrigerate for 30 minutes or more. Grill the fish until opaque halfway through. Turn the fish. Place the pineapple rings on the grill. Cook the fish until cooked through. Top each fillet with a pineapple ring. Serve hot. *Yield varies.*

# Pearl's Striped Bass

4 to 6 pounds striped bass fillets
6 slices cooked bacon
8 slices toast, or 2 cups
   bread crumbs
1 teaspoon pepper
1 teaspoon oregano
1 teaspoon chopped parsley

$1/2$ cup chopped almonds
$1/2$ cup olive oil
1 cup chopped celery
1 cup chopped onion
$1/2$ cup chopped red bell pepper
$1/2$ cup chopped green
   bell pepper

Preheat the oven to 400 degrees. Lightly grease a 9x13-inch baking dish. Arrange the fish evenly in 1 layer in the dish. Crumble the bacon and bread into a large bowl. Add the pepper, herbs and almonds and mix well.

Heat the oil in a skillet and sauté the celery, onion and bell peppers until the onion is translucent. Add to the bread crumb mixture. Press the bread mixture over the fillets. Bake, uncovered, for 15 minutes. Reduce heat to 350 degrees and bake for 40 minutes longer, covering with foil if needed to prevent overbrowning. *Makes 8 to 10 servings.*

# Grilled Bass

$1/4$ cup ($1/2$ stick) butter
Juice of 1 lemon
Juice of 1 lime
3 pounds bass with ribcage

Cajun seasoning or freshly
   ground pepper
Finely chopped fresh garlic
Whole fresh basil leaves

Melt the butter and add the lemon and lime juices and mix well. Pour over the fish. Season well. Sprinkle garlic over each fish and top with a basil leaf. Refrigerate for 30 minutes.

Heat a grill pan or similar appliance and grill the fillets for 4 to 6 minutes or until the fish flakes easily. Serve with boiled new potatoes in garlic-butter sauce, fresh green beans and corn bread. *Makes 4 servings.*

# FRIED STRIPER

6 to 8 pounds striper fillets
1 quart hot red pepper sauce
2¹/₂ pounds self-rising flour
Peanut oil

Cover the fish with hot pepper sauce and marinate for at least 2 hours. Coat each fillet in flour.

Heat oil to 300 degrees in a deep fryer or skillet. Deep-fry the fish until golden brown. Drain on paper towels. *Makes 10 to 12 servings.*

# FRIED ASIAN CARP

2 pounds carp fillets, scored
Salt and freshly ground pepper
Commercial fry coating
Vegetable oil
Lemon wedges

Choose small fish, 1 to 5 pounds, which have fine bones that dissolve in hot oil. Season the fillets with salt and pepper and refrigerate for 1 hour. Coat with fry coating.

Heat the oil to 375 degrees in a Dutch oven or deep fryer. Fry the fish until golden brown. Serve with lemon wedges or in a sandwich. *Makes 4 servings.*

# SAVORY OR SWEET SMOKED ASIAN CARP

### SAVORY CARP
5 pounds bighead or silver carp
   steaks or fillets, skin on
1 cup coarse or kosher salt
1 cup sugar
1 tablespoon freshly ground
   pepper
1 bunch fresh baby dill

### SWEET CARP
1 cup coarse or kosher salt
1 tablespoon freshly ground
   pepper
1 cup packed brown sugar
4 cups apple juice
2 cinnamon sticks
5 pounds bighead or silver carp
   steaks or fillets, skin on

For savory carp, arrange the fillets or steaks on a nonreactive pan or tray. Coat both sides of each piece of fish with salt, sugar, pepper and dill. Cover with plastic wrap and refrigerate for at least 8 hours.

For sweet carp, combine all the ingredients except carp in a very large nonreactive bowl and mix until the brown sugar dissolves. Add the fish and mix well. Cover with plastic wrap and refrigerate for at least 8 hours.

Soak the wood chips in water for 1 hour before smoking. Light a fire in a smoker and let burn until coals are covered with a layer of white ash. Fill the smoker's water pan to create steam and prevent the fish from drying.

Remove the fish from the marinade. Place on wire racks in the refrigerator for 1 hour with a pan underneath to catch drippings. The fish will develop a slight glaze. Lightly oil the grill grate and position the marinated fish on the rack. Add a handful of smoking chips to the charcoal and close the cooker. Replenish the chips every 20 to 30 minutes. Most fish will cook in 2 to 4 hours, but this will vary with weather conditions and desired depth of smokiness. Finished fillets will have a golden honey to mahogany color, depending on personal preference and type of wood chips used. Cooked fish will flake easily and is opaque.

*Smoking is a good way to prepare larger fish of 5 to 30 pounds. The light, oily texture of the meat readily absorbs the smoke flavor, and smoking loosens the bones and allows for easy extraction. Smoked carp is comparable to smoked whitefish or salmon.*

## Poached Silver Salad Sandwich

2 pounds bighead or silver carp
   fillets without skin
1 lemon
Salt
Freshly ground black pepper

Chopped fresh baby dill
Mayonnaise
Minced celery
Red bell pepper slices
Yellow bell pepper slices

Place the fillets on squares of aluminum foil and squeeze the lemon over them. Season with salt and black pepper to taste and sprinkle with dill. Fold up the foil packet, but leave open at the top. Steam in a steamer until the fish is opaque and flakes easily with a fork.

Flake the fish with a fork into a bowl and combine with enough mayonnaise to bind, celery and bell peppers. Chill in the refrigerator. Serve on bread with sliced cucumber and cheese, lettuce, tomato and pickles. *Makes 6 sandwiches.*


## Sautéed Fillets with Citrus

2 small skinned fish fillets, fresh
   or saltwater
Bread crumbs (optional)

2 tablespoons butter
Grapefruit and orange sections
   (canned are fine)

Coat the fish with bread crumbs, if desired. Melt the butter in a medium skillet over medium heat and sauté the fish until brown. Serve with grapefruit and orange sections. This recipe may be cooked on an outdoor stove. *Makes 2 servings.*

# THAI-STYLE BROILED FISH

1- to 1½-pound red snapper, trout, bass or whitefish, cleaned and scaled
1 stalk lemongrass, minced
1 to 2 green onions, sliced
1 lemon
1 tablespoon sugar
½ teaspoon salt
½ teaspoon ground white pepper
½ tablespoon grated fresh gingerroot
Sliced green onions

Make a series of vertical cuts in the fish to allow the marinade to penetrate. Place the fish in a nonreactive container, such as a glass baking dish or plastic bowl. Combine the lemongrass and green onions. Squeeze the lemon juice over the lemongrass mixture and add the sugar, salt, pepper and gingerroot and mix well. Pour the mixture over the fish and turn to coat both sides. Refrigerate for 45 to 60 minutes. Remove the fish from the marinade, discarding the marinade. Broil at 500 degrees for 2 to 3 minutes per side or until the fish becomes opaque and flakes easily with a fork. Garnish with sliced green onions and serve with Thai chili sauce, steamed rice and vegetables. *Makes 2 servings.*

"Fish taken out of the water and fried on the riverbank are
many times more delicious than those bought at the supermarket.
An oak fire, the smell of pine woods, the soft breeze—all seem to
add flavor that cannot be obtained under a roof."
—Charlie Elliott, *Gone Fishin'*

WILD FARE &
WISE WORDS

# VENISON

# VENISON

Anyone interested in enjoying the tempting taste of venison likely
lives within a reasonable distance of places where deer can be hunted. To a
greater extent perhaps than any other game animal, hunting is an imperative
when it comes to managing whitetail populations. That means, in effect, that
over much of the deer's range you are actually doing yourself and nature a favor by
hunting deer. More to the point, in the present context, is the fact that properly
dressed, handled, and prepared deer is as tasty as the animal is abundant.
The size of the animal ensures that it has the potential to make a major
contribution to the table fare we all, as hunters, enjoy.

While a successful quest brings a real sense of accomplishment, for the sensitive
and sensible hunter the decisive moment of truth is nonetheless a bittersweet one.
It is precisely at that point, though, as he contemplates his kill and perhaps
enjoys visions of venison dishes to come, that he should pause and ponder,
full of wonder, on the finality of the ultimate act in hunting. Theodore Roosevelt,
an avid outdoorsman and conservationist, as well as one of our great presidents,
captured the essence of the situation in *The Wilderness Hunter*:

*In hunting, the finding and killing of the game is after all but a part of the whole. The free,
self-reliant, adventurous life, with its rugged and stalwart democracy; the wild surroundings, the
grand beauty of the scenery; the chance to study the ways and habits of the woodland creatures—
all these unite to give to the career of the wilderness hunter its peculiar charm. The chase is
among the best of all national pastimes; it cultivates that vigorous manliness for the lack of which
in a nation, as in an individual, the possession of no other qualities can possibly atone.*

Don't overlook the health benefits of venison. It is often the only red meat heart
patients should eat. Additionally, it has never known the inoculants, vitamin
supplements, growth hormones, questionable feeding practices, and crowded
conditions endemic to both the beef and poultry industries. Venison has
much less fat than beef (and what is present should be removed when the
animal is processed), lower levels of cholesterol, and top-drawer nutritional value.
In short, venison is not only good; it is good for you.

# SMOKED VENISON HAM OR ROAST

1 (4- to 8-pound) boneless
    ham, muscle casing trimmed
Dale's seasoning
2 tablespoons oregano or Italian
    seasoning

$^{1}/_{2}$ tablespoon thyme
$^{1}/_{2}$ to 1 tablespoon rosemary
Salt and pepper to taste

Prick the meat all over with a fork. Rub with Dale's seasoning. Combine the remaining ingredients and rub into the meat. Let stand, covered, for 1 to 6 hours.

Grill the roast over direct heat until brown, then cook over indirect heat for 1 to $1^{1}/_{2}$ hours or until the meat reaches an internal temperature of about 160 degrees. Remove the meat to a charcoal or electric smoker and smoke for 2 hours.

*If you like, tenderize the meat with meat tenderizer, or soak it in cola for several hours before rubbing it with the seasonings.*

# SLOW COOKER ROAST WITH CRANBERRIES

1 ($10^{1}/_{2}$-ounce) can double-
    strength beef broth
$^{1}/_{2}$ can water
2 to 3 teaspoons cream-style
    prepared horseradish

$^{1}/_{4}$ teaspoon ground cinnamon
1 (16-ounce) can whole
    cranberry sauce
1 (3- to 4-pound) venison roast
Salt and pepper to taste

Combine the first 5 ingredients in a medium saucepan. Bring to a boil, stirring constantly. Pour over the venison roast in the slow cooker. Season with salt and pepper. Cook on Low for 6 to 8 hours or until the meat is tender. Pass the cooking liquid with the roast.

*Leftover roast makes delicious sandwiches.*

# BARBECUE ROAST

1 (3-pound) deer rump roast
Milk
1 teaspoon salt
1/2 teaspoon pepper
1/4 cup firmly packed brown
   sugar, divided
2 cups water
2 cups ketchup

3/4 cup cola soft drink
1/4 cup liquid smoke flavoring
2 tablespoons white vinegar
2 tablespoons Worcestershire
   sauce
1 tablespoon prepared mustard
1/2 teaspoon hot pepper sauce
Hamburger buns

Place the roast in a bowl or dish and pour in enough milk to come halfway up the roast. Cover and let soak for 8 hours or more, refrigerated. Remove the roast from the milk and discard the milk. Sprinkle the roast with salt and pepper and rub with 2 tablespoons of the brown sugar. Place the roast in a slow cooker and cook for 10 hours. Remove the roast and shred the meat.

Combine the remaining brown sugar and next 8 ingredients in a saucepan and bring to a boil. Reduce heat and simmer until thickened, about 15 minutes. Combine with the shredded meat. Serve the meat on hamburger buns. Note: Before soaking the meat, tenderize with Jaccard® meat tenderizer. You may also wish to brush the meat with Kitchen Bouquet before sprinkling with salt and pepper.

# MARINATED VENISON LOIN

Loin of venison
Italian dressing
Soy sauce

Teriyaki sauce
Garlic salt
Pepper

Cover the meat with Italian dressing, soy sauce and teriyaki sauce in a nonreactive container, such as a glass baking dish or plastic bowl. Refrigerate for at least 1 hour and up to 24 hours. Remove the meat from the marinade and grill until medium-rare. Season with garlic salt and pepper. Slice to serve.

# Venison Shoulder Roast with Vegetables

1 (5- to 7-pound) venison
   shoulder roast
Kosher or other coarse salt
Freshly ground pepper
6 tablespoons olive oil, divided
2 large red or other sweet onions,
   cut into halves
8 to 12 ounces carrots, cut into
   2-inch pieces

8 to 12 ounces celery stalks,
   cut into 2-inch pieces
2 whole red bell peppers,
   cut into halves
2 cups port wine
2 cups beef broth
6 garlic cloves, chopped
2 tablespoons butter

Preheat the oven to 325 degrees. Generously season the meat with salt and pepper. Heat 1/4 cup of the olive oil in a large skillet or Dutch oven over medium-high heat. Sear the roast thoroughly on all sides. Reserve the pan juices.

Remove the roast to a roasting pan. Add the onions, carrots, celery, red bell peppers, wine and beef broth to the roasting pan. Heat the remaining 2 tablespoons olive oil with the pan juices. Sauté the garlic in the liquid. Use this mixture to baste the roast.

Cover the pan with a lid or foil. Roast, basting every 30 to 45 minutes. Cook to desired doneness, from 1 1/2 to 3 hours: 140 degrees for rare, 145 degrees medium-rare, 160 degrees for medium and 170 degrees for well done. Generally, the longer the meat cooks, the more tender the result.

Remove from the oven when the meat reaches the desired internal temperature and let stand; the meat will continue to cook.

Drain the pan juices and bring to a boil in a saucepan. Boil until the liquid is reduced to 1 to 1 1/2 cups. Add the butter to the pan juices.

Slice the roast and coat lightly with sauce. Serve with an orange-cranberry sauce and the vegetables. *Makes 4 to 8 servings.*

# Venison Osso Buco

2 tablespoons olive oil
3 pounds venison roast, cut
   1$^1$/$_2$ inches thick
$^1$/$_2$ teaspoon kosher salt
$^1$/$_4$ teaspoon freshly ground
   pepper
1 onion, chopped
1 carrot, diced
1 celery stalk, diced
$^1$/$_2$ cup dry white wine
1 (15-ounce) can tomatoes in
   juice, drained and chopped
   (reserve $^1$/$_2$ cup juice)

1 (14-ounce) can beef broth
1 teaspoon beef base
$^1$/$_2$ teaspoon basil
$^1$/$_2$ teaspoon rosemary
$^1$/$_4$ teaspoon thyme
2 bay leaves

GREMOLATA
2 tablespoons chopped fresh
   parsley
Grated zest of 1 lemon
1 garlic clove, minced

Heat 1 tablespoon of the oil in a Dutch oven over medium-high heat. Add the venison in batches and brown. Remove to a platter and season with salt and pepper.

Heat the remaining oil and sauté the onion, carrot and celery, stirring occasionally, until softened, about 3 minutes. Stir in the wine and cook until almost evaporated. Add the tomatoes, reserved juice, beef broth, beef base and herbs. Return the venison to the Dutch oven and bring to a boil. Cover and reduce heat; simmer until fork-tender, about 2 to 2$^1$/$_2$ hours. Remove the lid during the last 30 minutes for the sauce to thicken. Taste and adjust seasonings.

For the gremolata, combine the parsley, lemon zest and garlic in a bowl.

Arrange the venison on a deep serving platter and pour the sauce over it. Sprinkle with gremolata and serve with rice or pasta. *Makes 6 to 8 servings.*

# Venison Wellington

1 venison tenderloin, about
  2 pounds
Salt and pepper to taste
4 tablespoons olive oil
1/2 cup chopped onion
1 pound porcini or portobello
  mushrooms, finely chopped

1 tablespoon chopped garlic
1/2 cup madeira
1/4 to 1/2 pound mushroom pâté
1 pound frozen puff pastry
1 egg, beaten with
  1 tablespoon water

Preheat the oven to 350 degrees. Season the tenderloin with salt and pepper. Heat 3 tablespoons of the oil in a large skillet. Sear the tenderloin on all sides. Remove from heat and cool. Heat remaining 1 tablespoon oil in the same skillet and sauté the onion, mushrooms and garlic until tender. Add the wine and simmer until it is evaporated. Remove from heat and cool. Spread the pâté over the tenderloin. Top with the vegetable mixture. Roll the puff pastry into a rectangle that will encase the tenderloin. Brush edges of the dough with some of the egg mixture and press to seal. Decorate with extra dough and brush the surface with egg mixture. Bake for about 30 to 35 minutes or until the pastry is golden brown. *Makes 2 to 4 servings.*

# Ginger Steak

1/2 cup orange juice
1/2 cup teriyaki sauce or
  marinade

1 teaspoon ground ginger
1 pound venison steaks,
  cut 3/4 inch thick

Combine the orange juice, teriyaki sauce and ginger in a sealable plastic bag and add the steaks. Seal, pressing out air, and refrigerate for 24 hours, turning the bag occasionally. Drain the marinade and grill the steak to medium-rare, taking care not to overcook. *Makes 4 servings.*

*If it's not possible to cook the steaks after the 24 hours of marinating time, they may be frozen and cooked later.*

# Venison Loin Steak in Brandy Cream Sauce

2 tablespoons (or more) liquid margarine
2 (8- to 10-ounce) venison loin steaks, cut 1 inch thick
3 small slices onion, separated into rings
1/4 cup sliced mushrooms
1 cup evaporated milk (or a combination of a 5-ounce can plus 3 ounces fresh milk)
2 tablespoons brandy
1/2 to 1 tablespoon salt

Heat the margarine in a saucepan and cook the venison, onion and mushrooms until the steak is just pink inside and the mushrooms and onion are tender. Remove the steak and vegetables and set aside.

Add the milk, brandy and salt to the pan juices. Cook, stirring constantly, until the mixture is thickened and reduced by half. Return the mushrooms and onion to the pan to reheat. Pour the sauce over the steaks. Serve with roasted potatoes, fresh broccoli and fruit salad. *Makes 2 servings.*

# Broiled Venison Steaks with Parsley Butter

Venison loin, cut into 1-inch steaks
1/2 cup (1 stick) butter, softened
1/2 teaspoon salt
Dash of pepper
1/4 teaspoon chopped fresh parsley
3/4 tablespoon lemon juice

Preheat the broiler and broil the steaks 3 inches from the flame until nicely browned, about 5 minutes. Turn and broil the other side. Venison should be pink in the middle but well browned on the surface.

Combine the butter, salt, pepper and parsley in a bowl and mix well. Add the lemon juice slowly, working it into the mixture. Use right away or chill. Serve each steak with a spoonful of parsley butter.

# Venison Steaks with
# Shrimp and Asparagus Sauce

1 pound asparagus
1 package béarnaise sauce mix (or prepare sauce from scratch)
1 tablespoon butter
2 tablespoons olive oil
Several sliced green onions
1 pound venison loin steaks
1/4 cup all-purpose flour
1/2 pound shrimp, cooked, peeled and chopped

Steam the asparagus until tender-crisp, then drop into ice water to stop cooking. Prepare the béarnaise sauce according to the package directions.

Melt the butter with the olive oil in a nonstick skillet and sauté the green onions until tender. Drain and add to the béarnaise.

Flatten the steaks with a meat mallet until very thin. Coat with flour and brown quickly in the drippings in the skillet. Add the shrimp and asparagus to the béarnaise and heat gently.

Serve the steaks topped with shrimp and asparagus sauce. Serve with garlic smashed potatoes or oregano roasted potatoes. *Makes 2 to 4 servings.*

"I have a philosophy which teaches me that certain game birds and animals are apparently made to be hunted, because of their peculiar food value and because their character lends zest to the pursuit of them. It has never seemed to me to be too far-fetched to suppose that Providence placed game here for a special purpose."
—Archibald Rutledge, *An American Hunter*

# STEAKS WITH CRAB, SHRIMP AND SCALLOP SAUCE

CRAB, SHRIMP AND
SCALLOP SAUCE
2 tablespoons olive oil
8 ounces sliced fresh mushrooms
2 cups heavy cream
1/4 cup white zinfandel
Salt and pepper to taste
1/4 cup (1/2 stick) butter,
 cut into 12 pieces
1/2 pound crab meat

8 to 12 medium shrimp, cooked
 and shelled
6 to 8 sea scallops, cooked and
 chopped

STEAKS
1 tablespoon olive oil
1 tablespoon margarine
1 pound loin steaks,
 cut 1/2 inch thick

For the sauce, heat the olive oil in a large skillet over medium-high heat.
Sauté the mushrooms for 5 minutes. Add the cream and wine and cook
until reduced and thick, about 10 to 12 minutes. Season with salt and
pepper. Stir in the butter, 1 piece at a time, incorporating each piece
completely before adding the next. Stir in the crab meat, shrimp and
scallops and heat through.

For the steaks, heat the olive oil and margarine in a large skillet over
medium-high heat. Cook the steaks to medium-rare. Keep steaks warm
on a platter while finishing the sauce. Serve the sauce over the steaks.
*Makes 4 servings.*

# Venison Steaks with Shrimp Gravy over Garlic Cheese Grits

**STEAKS**
1 pound venison loin steaks
2 tablespoons olive oil
1 teaspoon lemon and lime
  pepper seasoning

**SHRIMP GRAVY**
4 slices bacon
1 onion, chopped
1 pound peeled and deveined
  shrimp
$1^1/_2$ teaspoons Worcestershire
  sauce
$^1/_4$ teaspoon kosher salt
$^1/_8$ teaspoon freshly ground
  pepper

2 tablespoons all-purpose flour
1 cup water

**GARLIC CHEESE GRITS**
1 cup chicken broth
$^1/_2$ cup half-and-half
$^1/_2$ cup water
$^1/_4$ cup ($^1/_2$ stick) butter
1 garlic clove, minced
$^1/_2$ teaspoon kosher salt
$^1/_4$ teaspoon freshly ground
  pepper
1 cup quick-cooking grits
$^3/_4$ cup shredded Cheddar
  cheese

For the steaks, drizzle the steaks with olive oil and sprinkle with seasoning. Let the steaks marinate for 1 hour.

For the shrimp gravy, cook the bacon in the skillet until crisp, then remove. Cook the steaks in the bacon drippings, then remove from the skillet. Cover the steaks with foil and let rest.

Sauté the onion in the bacon drippings. Add the well-drained shrimp, Worcestershire sauce, salt and pepper, stirring constantly. When the shrimp begin to turn pink, sprinkle the flour over the shrimp. Add the water and cook until the gravy is the desired consistency, stirring constantly. Crumble the bacon and add to the sauce. Simmer for 4 minutes.

For the grits, bring the first 7 ingredients to a boil in a large saucepan over medium heat. Stir in the grits, cover, and reduce heat to low. Cook, stirring often, for 5 to 6 minutes. Remove from heat, add the cheese and stir to mix well. Place a mound of grits on each plate, top with steak and spoon shrimp gravy over all. Serve immediately. *Makes 4 to 6 servings.*

# VENISON WITH
# LOBSTER CREAM SAUCE

LOBSTER CREAM SAUCE
2 tablespoons butter
2 tablespoons minced onion
3 tablespoons all-purpose flour
1/2 cup white wine
1/2 cup heavy cream
1 1/2 cups milk
1/8 teaspoon allspice
Salt to taste
1/2 teaspoon pepper
8 ounces real or imitation
  lobster meat

STEAKS
2 tablespoons butter
2 tablespoons olive oil
1/4 to 1/2 cup all-purpose flour
Salt and pepper to taste
8 venison steaks, pounded thin
Juice of 1 lemon

For the sauce, melt the butter in a saucepan over medium heat and sauté the onion until tender. Add the flour and mix well. Gradually add the wine, cream and milk, stirring constantly. Add the allspice, salt and pepper and simmer, stirring constantly, until thick. Stir in the lobster.

For the steaks, heat the butter and oil in a skillet. Combine the flour with salt and pepper. Dip the steak in the flour and cook for 2 to 3 minutes on each side. Turn, sprinkle with lemon juice and cook until brown outside but pink inside. Serve steaks topped with lobster sauce. *Makes 8 servings.*

"If there is a sport that whets the appetite
more keenly than deer hunting, I do not know it."
—Archibald Rutledge, *My Colonel and His Lady*

# LOIN STEAKS WITH
# APRICOT MUSTARD SAUCE

Salt to taste
4 to 6 venison loin steaks
Pepper to taste
Butter

APRICOT MUSTARD SAUCE
$1/2$ cup grainy brown mustard
$1/3$ cup apricot jam
$1/4$ cup brandy

Heat a nonstick skillet over medium-high heat; sprinkle the skillet lightly with salt and add the steaks. Cook until brown. Lift the steaks and sprinkle the skillet with more salt. Cook the other side of the steaks. Season the cooked steaks with pepper and top with a pat of butter. Let the butter melt before removing the steak from the pan.

For the sauce, heat the mustard, jam and brandy in a small saucepan over medium heat, stirring frequently, until the jam has melted and the ingredients are well combined. Drizzle the sauce over the steaks and serve immediately. *Makes 4 servings.*

# BLUEBERRY BACKSTRAP

2 tablespoons butter
4 venison loin steaks,
   cut $1/2$ inch thick
Juice and zest of 1 large lemon
1 cup chicken broth
$1/2$ cup butter

1 cup fresh or frozen blueberries
Several dashes of ground
   cinnamon
Several dashes of ground ginger
Salt and freshly ground pepper
   to taste

Melt 2 tablespoons butter in a large skillet and cook the steaks until brown on both sides and cooked medium-rare. Remove to a platter and keep warm. Pour the lemon juice, zest and chicken broth into the skillet and bring to a boil. Cook until the mixture is reduced to about $1/2$ cup. Lower heat to medium and whisk in $1/4$ cup butter, 1 tablespoon at a time. Stir in the blueberries, cinnamon, ginger, salt and pepper. Serve the sauce over the steaks. *Makes 4 servings.*

# Backstrap in Bacon

1/2 cup Dale's steak
   seasoning
1/2 cup water

1 pound venison loin, cut into
   1-inch chunks
Bacon slices, cut into halves

Combine the steak seasoning and water in a large bowl. Add the meat and stir to coat. Cover and refrigerate for 6 to 8 hours, stirring occasionally.
   Soak a handful of wooden picks, 1 for each chunk of venison, in water for 30 minutes. Prepare the grill for direct grilling over medium heat. Drain the meat and discard the marinade. Wrap each piece of meat in bacon and secure with a wooden pick. Grill for 8 to 10 minutes or until the center of the meat is just pink. Serve hot. *Makes 4 servings.*

*Dale's seasoning is based on a soy sauce blend and is usually available in the South and Southeast. If you can't find it in your area, visit www.dalesseasoning.com.*

# Venison Loin Medallions

1 cup low-salt chicken broth
1 cup beef broth
1/2 cup cherry liqueur
1/3 cup cherry pie filling
1 tablespoon cornstarch
   dissolved in 1/4 cup water

3 tablespoons butter
Salt and pepper to taste
8 venison loin steak medallions,
   cut about 1/2-inch thick

Bring the chicken and beef broths to a boil in a small heavy saucepan. Boil until the liquid is reduced to 1 cup. Add the cherry liqueur and boil until the liquid is reduced to 3/4 cup. Whisk in the pie filling and simmer until the sauce begins to thicken. Stir in the cornstarch mixture and cook until the sauce thickens, stirring. Whisk in 1 tablespoon of the butter. Season with salt and pepper and set aside. Sprinkle the venison with salt and pepper. Melt the remaining butter in a large nonstick skillet over medium-high heat and cook the venison to desired doneness. Place 2 medallions on each plate and top with the sauce. *Makes 4 servings.*

# Fajita Salad with Caramelized Onion

### Steak

1 pound venison loin steak, trimmed
1/4 cup ketchup
1/4 cup fresh lime juice
1/4 teaspoon lime zest
2 tablespoons honey
2 tablespoons minced green onions
2 tablespoons olive oil
2 tablespoons water
1/4 teaspoon red pepper flakes
1/4 teaspoon ground cumin
1/2 teaspoon kosher salt, or to taste

### Caramelized Onion

1 tablespoon olive oil
1 supersweet onion, thinly sliced
1 pinch of sugar

### Salad

1 (10-ounce) bag romaine and leaf lettuce mix
1 cup grape tomatoes, cut into halves
1 avocado, chopped
1 cup sliced cucumber
1/2 cup sliced fresh mushrooms
1 cup grated Cheddar cheese
1 (2 1/4-ounce) can sliced black olives
1 1/2 cups corn chips, coarsely crumbled
1 (14-ounce) can pinto beans, drained and rinsed
1/4 cup sliced green onions
1/4 cup sour cream

For the steak, place the steak in a glass dish. Combine the ketchup, lime juice, lime zest, honey, green onions, olive oil, water, red pepper flakes, cumin and kosher salt in a measuring cup and mix well. Pour 1/4 cup of the dressing over the steak, turning to coat. Marinate for at least 15 minutes or up to 2 hours, refrigerating after 30 minutes.

For the caramelized onion, heat 1 tablespoon olive oil in a skillet over medium-high heat. Add the onion and sugar and cook over low heat until dark golden brown, about 15 to 20 minutes. Drain on paper towels.

Remove the steak from the marinade and pat dry. Season with salt and pepper. Sear the steak in a hot skillet on both sides until brown on both sides, 3 to 4 minutes per side. (You may broil or grill the steak, if preferred, or use a grilling pan.) Let stand for 5 minutes. Slice thinly across the grain.

To assemble, layer half the salad greens, grape tomatoes, avocado, cucumber, mushrooms, cheese, black olives, corn chips, pinto beans, green onions, steak and caramelized onion in a deep glass bowl. (A 12-inch trifle bowl is ideal.) Drizzle half the remaining dressing over the layers. Repeat the layers. Top with the sour cream. *Makes 4 servings.*

## London Broil

1/4 cup canola oil
1/4 cup lemon juice
2 tablespoons soy sauce
2 teaspoons sugar

2 garlic cloves, minced
1 venison flank steak, 1 1/2 to
2 pounds

Combine the oil, lemon juice, soy sauce, sugar and garlic in a bowl and whisk to combine. Pour over the steak in a glass baking dish or plastic bowl. Cover and refrigerate for 4 to 8 hours, turning occasionally. Prepare the grill for direct medium heat and oil the grate. Drain the steak and discard the marinade. Grill the steak to desired doneness, turning once, about 12 to 14 minutes total. Let stand for 5 minutes, then slice thinly across the grain. *Makes 4 to 6 servings.*

# BROILED VENISON CHOPS

6 venison chops, cut 1 inch thick
Worcestershire sauce
Garlic salt

Salt and pepper to taste
1/4 cup melted butter
Parsley sprigs

Trim fat from the chops and wipe with a clean damp cloth. Sprinkle each chop with Worcestershire sauce and season with garlic salt, salt and pepper. Sauté the chops on both sides in melted butter in a hot cast-iron skillet, then cook, uncovered, over medium heat, until the chops are medium-rare. Serve hot, drizzled with additional butter, and garnish with parsley. *Makes 6 servings.*

# SWEET VENISON KABOBS

4 to 5 pounds venison loin
1 cup soy sauce
1 cup packed brown sugar
1/2 cup olive oil
3 (6-ounce) jars whole button
 mushrooms

Cherry tomatoes
2 (20-ounce) cans pineapple
 chunks

Cut the meat into bite-size cubes. Combine the soy sauce, brown sugar and olive oil in a saucepan and heat, stirring, until the brown sugar dissolves; do not boil. Pour over the venison cubes and refrigerate for 4 to 6 hours.

Thread the meat, mushrooms, tomatoes and pineapple alternately onto skewers. Grill over charcoal or on a gas grill for about 30 minutes, turning occasionally. Good with yellow rice and a green salad. *Makes 8 servings.*

# CRUMB-COATED VENISON

1 sleeve saltine crackers, crushed
1 1/2 cups self-rising flour
1 teaspoon pepper

1 pound cubed venison
1 cup 2% milk
2 to 4 tablespoons vegetable oil

Combine the crumbs, flour and pepper. Dip the venison into the milk, then coat with the crumb mixture. Heat the oil to 380 degrees in a skillet and cook the venison for 10 minutes or until golden brown, turning occasionally. Drain on paper towels. *Makes 2 to 4 servings.*

# VENISON CUBED STEAK AND GRAVY

2 pounds venison cubed steaks
1 cup buttermilk
1 1/2 to 2 cups all-purpose flour
Salt and pepper to taste
1/4 to 1/2 cup vegetable oil

1 onion, sliced (optional)
3 tablespoons all-purpose flour
1 cup milk
1 cup water

Preheat the oven to 350 degrees. Cut the steak into serving pieces and marinate in the buttermilk for a few minutes. Season 1 1/2 to 2 cups flour with salt and pepper. Heat the oil in a large ovenproof skillet or Dutch oven. Coat the meat with the flour and fry in the oil until golden brown. Drain on paper towels.

Pour off all but 2 to 3 tablespoons oil. Sauté the onion in the remaining oil until tender. Sift 3 tablespoons of flour over the onion and oil and cook, stirring, until the flour is brown. Remove from heat and add the meat, milk and water and mix well. Cover the pan and bake for 30 to 40 minutes, checking often after 25 minutes and adding water if the gravy becomes too thick. Serve the meat and gravy over rice or mashed potatoes. *Makes 8 to 10 servings.*

# CUBED STEAKS IN MUSHROOM GRAVY

STEAKS
1/2 cup all-purpose flour
1 teaspoon garlic salt
1/4 teaspoon coarsely ground
   pepper
1 cup canola oil
2 pounds cubed venison steaks

MUSHROOM GRAVY
8 ounces sliced mushrooms
1/2 cup sliced onion
2 tablespoons all-purpose flour
2 (10-ounce) cans beef
   consommé
1/4 cup water

Combine the flour, garlic salt and pepper. Coat the meat with the flour mixture. Heat the oil in a large skillet over medium-high heat until a pinch of flour dropped into the oil sizzles. Fry the steaks until brown on both sides. Drain on paper towels.

Drain all but 3 tablespoons of the oil, leaving the brown bits in the skillet. Sauté the mushrooms and onion in the oil. Add the flour and mix well. Stir in the consommé and water and cook, stirring until well blended. Add the steak to the gravy. Cover and lower the heat to simmer. Cook for 1 to 1 1/2 hours. Serve with hot cooked rice and butter beans. *Makes 4 to 6 servings.*

"I fully realize that not all men who roam the fields and woods with guns
are good men; indeed, many may be good shots, yet hardly worth knowing.
But there are many thousands of men in our country who fulfill my idea of
what good hunters should be; and among the memories that I would
exchange for no others are my recollections of these friends."
—Archibald Rutledge, *Hunter's Choice*

# CHICKEN-FRIED STEAK

STEAKS
1 pound cubed venison steaks
$1/4$ teaspoon kosher salt
$1/4$ teaspoon freshly ground
    black pepper
1 sleeve saltine crackers, crushed
1 cup all-purpose flour
$1/2$ teaspoon baking powder
$1/2$ teaspoon freshly ground
    black pepper

Several dashes of ground
    red pepper
2 eggs
$3/4$ cup milk

GRAVY
6 to 8 tablespoons canola oil
4 tablespoons all-purpose flour
2 cups milk

Sprinkle the steaks with salt and $1/4$ teaspoon pepper. Combine the cracker crumbs, flour, baking powder, $1/2$ teaspoon black pepper and red pepper and mix well. Beat the eggs with the milk. Dip the steak in the crumb mixture, then into the milk. Coat with more crumb mixture, pressing the crumbs into the meat.

Heat the oil to medium-hot in a large cast-iron skillet. Fry the steaks until brown on both sides, turning once. Keep the steaks warm in a 225-degree oven.

Pour off all but 4 tablespoons oil in the skillet, leaving the brown bits. Stir in the flour and cook over medium heat, stirring, until brown. Remove from heat and stir in the milk. Return to heat and cook, stirring constantly, until the mixture is thickened. Sprinkle with parsley, if desired. Serve the gravy with the steaks and mashed potatoes. *Makes 2 to 4 servings.*

# CHILI STEAK AND SALSA

1 teaspoon chili powder
1 or 2 garlic cloves, minced
1/2 teaspoon kosher salt
1/2 teaspoon pepper

3/4 to 1 pound cubed
    venison steaks
1 tablespoon olive oil
Fresh Salsa (below)

Combine the chili powder, garlic, salt and pepper and mix well. Rub evenly into both sides of the steaks. Heat the oil in a nonstick skillet over medium heat until hot. Add the steaks and cook, turning once, to desired degree of doneness, about 8 minutes. Serve with the salsa. *Makes 2 to 3 servings.*

# FRESH SALSA

2 large tomatoes, chopped
2 tablespoons minced fresh
    cilantro
1/2 cup thinly sliced
    green onions
1 fresh jalapeño pepper, seeded
    and finely chopped

1 garlic clove, minced
2 tablespoons olive oil
3 tablespoons fresh lime juice
1/2 teaspoon salt
1/8 teaspoon black pepper

Combine the tomatoes, cilantro, green onions, jalapeño pepper, garlic, olive oil, lime juice, salt and black pepper in a large bowl and mix well. Cover and refrigerate for several hours for the flavors to blend. *Makes 2 to 3 cups.*

# Cubed Steak Italiano

2 tablespoons olive oil
1 pound cubed venison steaks,
   cut into strips
1 onion, sliced
1 green bell pepper, cut into
   strips
1 garlic clove, minced
1 cup sliced mushrooms
1 (25-ounce) jar meatless
   spaghetti sauce
1 teaspoon dried basil
Salt and pepper to taste

Heat the olive oil in a large skillet and sauté the steak, onion, bell pepper, garlic and mushrooms until tender. Stir in the spaghetti sauce, basil, salt and pepper. Cover and simmer for 15 to 30 minutes to blend the flavors. Serve over pasta. *Makes 4 servings.*

# Pizza Venison Swiss Steak

1/3 cup all-purpose flour
1/2 teaspoon salt
1/4 teaspoon pepper
1 pound cubed venison steak
3 tablespoons olive oil
1 onion, sliced
1 cup fresh mushrooms, sliced
1 (15-ounce) jar pizza sauce
1/4 cup water
1 bay leaf
1/4 teaspoon oregano
1/4 teaspoon basil
1/4 teaspoon Italian seasoning
1/2 to 1 cup shredded
   mozzarella cheese

Combine the flour, salt and pepper. Coat the steak with the flour mixture. Heat the oil in a skillet and brown the steaks, in batches if needed, over high heat, 1 to 2 minutes for each side. Remove the steaks to a greased 9x13-inch baking dish.

Preheat the oven to 350 degrees. Sauté the onion and mushrooms in the skillet over medium heat until tender. Stir in the pizza sauce, water and herbs. Bring to a boil and pour over the steak. Bake, covered, for 45 minutes. Uncover and sprinkle with the cheese. Return to the oven until the cheese is melted. Serve with pasta, salad and Texas toast. *Makes 4 to 6 servings.*

# Oven Swiss Steak

3/4 to 1 pound boneless venison
    cubed steak
3 tablespoons flour
1/2 teaspoon salt
2 tablespoons olive oil
1 (14-ounce) can tomatoes

1/2 cup chopped celery
1/2 cup chopped carrots
2 tablespoons chopped onion
1 teaspoon Worcestershire sauce
1/4 cup shredded
    Cheddar cheese

Preheat the oven to 350 degrees. Cut the meat into 2 portions. Combine the flour and salt on a plate. Coat the meat with the flour mixture. Heat the oil in a large skillet and brown the steaks. Arrange the venison in a 7x11-inch baking dish. Add the flour to the drippings in the skillet and mix well. Add the tomatoes, celery, carrots, onion and Worcestershire sauce to the skillet. Cook, stirring constantly, until the mixture boils. Pour over the meat. Cover and bake until the meat and vegetables are tender, about 1 hour. Sprinkle with the cheese and bake until the cheese is melted. Serve with pasta and vegetable salad. *Makes 2 servings.*

# Thai-Style Venison Salad

1/2 pound venison steak
1 red or yellow onion,
    thinly sliced
1/2 cucumber, thinly sliced
1 stalk lemongrass, thinly sliced
1 green onion, thinly sliced

1 teaspoon sugar
2 ounces fish sauce
Juice of 2 limes
1 teaspoon chili oil
Cilantro
Red or Thai chile peppers

Grill or pan-fry the steak until medium-rare. Let cool slightly, then cut into 1/8-inch slices. Combine the onion, cucumber, lemongrass and green onion in a bowl and mix well. Combine the sugar, fish sauce, lime juice and chili oil in a separate bowl. Top the vegetables with the meat and drizzle with the dressing. Refrigerate to chill and to allow the flavors to blend. Garnish with cilantro and chile peppers. *Makes 2 servings.*

# Venison Steak Fingers with Two Sauces

HONEY MUSTARD SAUCE
$1/3$ cup honey
$1^1/2$ cups mayonnaise
$1/4$ teaspoon freshly ground
   pepper
Dash of Worcestershire sauce
$1^1/2$ tablespoons prepared
   mustard
$1/8$ teaspoon kosher salt
$3/4$ teaspoon dried cilantro

CREOLE MUSTARD SAUCE
8 ounces sour cream
$1/4$ cup Creole mustard

1 tablespoon cider vinegar
1 teaspoon Cajun seasoning
Several dashes of
   hot pepper sauce

STEAK FINGERS
$1/2$ cup olive oil
$1/4$ cup red or white wine
1 teaspoon dried basil
$1/2$ teaspoon steak seasoning
1 pound venison steak,
   cut into strips
1 sleeve saltines, crushed
Olive oil

For the honey mustard sauce, combine the honey, mayonnaise, pepper, Worcestershire sauce, mustard, salt and cilantro in a medium bowl and mix well. Store in the refrigerator.

For the Creole mustard sauce, combine the sour cream, Creole mustard, vinegar, Cajun seasoning and hot pepper sauce in a medium bowl and mix well. Store in the refrigerator.

For the steak fingers, combine $1/2$ cup olive oil, wine, basil, steak seasoning and venison steak in a sealable plastic bag and refrigerate for 4 hours. Remove the steak from the plastic bag, discarding the marinade. Coat the steak with the crumbs. Heat olive oil in a large skillet and cook the steak until golden brown on the outside and pink in the center. Serve with mustard sauces. *Makes 4 servings.*

# Venison Bites

3 pounds venison
2 cups all-purpose flour
1 cup cornmeal
1 teaspoon Greek seasoning

1 teaspoon seasoned garlic salt
1 teaspoon paprika
1 teaspoon pepper
Oil for deep-frying

Cut the venison into bite-size pieces and soak in ice water for 30 minutes. Combine the flour, cornmeal, Greek seasoning, garlic salt, paprika and pepper on a plate or waxed paper. Drain the venison and coat with the flour mixture.

Heat oil to 375 degrees in a Dutch oven. Fry the venison bites until golden brown. Serve as an appetizer with spicy mustard or horseradish sauce or as a main dish. *Makes 6 main dish servings or 12 appetizer servings.*

# Souper Stew

2 pounds venison,
  cut into chunks
1 (10$^1/_2$-ounce) can cream of
  potato soup
1 (10$^1/_2$-ounce) can cream of
  mushroom soup

1 (10$^1/_2$-ounce) can cream of
  celery soup
1 envelope dry onion soup mix
1 soup can water

Arrange the venison in a Dutch oven. Combine the soups and the water and pour over the venison. Bring to a boil, reduce heat to a simmer and cook until tender, 1$^1/_2$ to 2 hours. Alternatively, cook in a slow cooker for 6 to 8 hours. Serve over rice or pasta. *Makes 6 to 8 servings.*

*Add potatoes, carrots, and peas to any leftover stew to "rerun" it for another meal, or use the leftovers as a base for venison vegetable soup.*

# Venison Stew

2 to 3 pounds venison roast
2 (10½-ounce) cans beef broth
1½ to 2 pounds potatoes, cubed
3 or 4 onions, quartered

8 ounces baby carrots
Salt and pepper to taste
Worcestershire sauce to taste

Cut the roast into 1-inch cubes. Combine in a Dutch oven with the beef broth. Simmer until the meat is nearly tender.

Preheat the oven to 350 degrees. Add the potatoes, onions and carrots to the pan and season with salt, pepper and Worcestershire sauce. Cover and bake for 1 hour or until the vegetables are very tender. *Makes 6 to 8 servings.*

# Simpleton Stew

1 pound venison stew meat
½ teaspoon ground ginger
1 teaspoon Season-All pepper
   seasoning
1 tablespoon soy or teriyaki
   sauce

1 (15-ounce) can potatoes
1 (8-ounce) can water chestnuts
1 (15-ounce) can French-cut
   green beans
1 (10½-ounce) can cream of
   mushroom soup

Combine the meat, ginger, pepper seasoning and soy sauce in a slow cooker. Cook on Low for 2 hours. Add the remaining ingredients and cook for 2 hours longer. Serve on its own or over wild rice. You can also use a venison roast, adjusting the time for the size. *Makes 8 servings.*

# Pressure Cooker Venison Pilaf

4 envelopes dry onion soup mix
4 cups water
4 to 5 pounds venison, cut into
  bite-size pieces
2 large onions
1/2 cup (1 stick) butter

2 (6-ounce) jars button
  mushrooms
1 teaspoon rosemary
Salt and pepper to taste
8 cups cooked rice

Combine the soup with 4 cups water in a pressure cooker. Add the venison and cook under pressure for 40 minutes. Chop the onions and sauté in the butter in a skillet until translucent. Add the next 6 ingredients to the venison. Heat through (not under pressure), adding more water if needed. Serve over hot cooked rice. *Makes 12 servings.*

*Good for guests because it can be prepared in advance and kept warm. The mixture can also be cooked in a slow cooker for several hours.*

# Venison Sausage Casserole

2 pounds bulk venison sausage
1 cup uncooked grits
4 cups water
4 tablespoons butter or
  margarine

2 cups grated Cheddar cheese
Salt and pepper to taste
1 1/2 cups milk
5 eggs

Preheat the oven to 350 degrees. Spray a 9x13-inch casserole with nonstick cooking spray. Brown the sausage in a large skillet, breaking up the large chunks; drain. Crumble the sausage over the bottom of the casserole. Cook the grits in the water according to the package directions. Grits should be thick rather than runny. Add the butter, cheese, salt and pepper and mix well. Beat the milk and eggs; stir into the grits mixture. Pour over the sausage. Bake for 1 hour. *Makes 8 servings.*

*Add some chopped red or green bell pepper for a taste of the Southwest.*

# GLAZED VENISON SAUSAGE

2 to 3 feet venison sausage,
  in casing
$^1/_2$ cup apple jelly

$^1/_2$ cup apple cider
2 teaspoons cornstarch

Grill the sausage until brown; turn and grill until it can be broken into 2- to 3-inch lengths with tongs. Place the pieces in a nonstick skillet on a side burner.

Combine the jelly with the cider until a thin consistency is reached. Heat in a small saucepan over low heat. Add the cornstarch and cook until thickened to a glaze consistency.

Pour the glaze into the skillet. Bring to a simmer and turn the sausage to coat. Serve hot.

# STEWED POTATOES AND SAUSAGE

$^1/_2$ cup (1 stick) butter, divided
1 white onion, chopped
$^1/_4$ cup diced bell pepper
$^1/_4$ cup diced celery
1 teaspoon minced garlic
2 teaspoons salt

1 tablespoon Cajun seasoning
8 large red potatoes, washed and
  chopped
1 pound deer summer sausage
6 cups water
1 bunch green onion tops, sliced

Melt $^1/_2$ of the butter in a heavy saucepan and sauté the onion, bell pepper, celery, garlic and seasonings over medium heat until tender. Add the potatoes, sausage and water. Bring to a boil and simmer for 30 minutes. Add the remaining 4 tablespoons butter and green onions. Let stand for 15 minutes and serve. *Makes 4 servings.*

# Taco Corn Bread Pizza

2 tablespoons olive oil, divided
1 (8.5-ounce) package corn bread mix
1 pound ground venison
$^1/_2$ to 1 (1.25-ounce) envelope taco seasoning mix
1 to 1$^1/_2$ cups shredded white Cheddar cheese
$^1/_2$ cup sliced black olives
Fresh cilantro, salsa, guacamole and sour cream for garnish

Preheat the oven to 400 degrees. Spread 1 tablespoon of the oil on a 12-inch pizza pan, coating thoroughly.

Prepare the corn bread mix using the package directions. Spread the batter on the prepared pan. Bake until light brown, about 8 to 10 minutes.

Heat the remaining olive oil in a skillet and cook the ground venison until brown and crumbly, stirring to break up the chunks. Add the taco seasoning mix and prepare according to the package directions. Simmer to reduce the liquid in the skillet.

Spread the corn bread crust with $^1/_2$ cup of the cheese. Spread the venison mixture over the cheese and top with the sliced olives and remaining cheese. Bake until the cheese is melted, 4 to 5 minutes. Top with garnishes.
*Makes 4 to 6 servings.*

*If you prefer a less spicy pizza, use only half the taco seasoning mix. Lawry's brand taco seasoning mix is particularly tasty with venison.*

# Swamp Chili

6 pounds ground venison
2 large onions, chopped
2 bell peppers, chopped
1/2 cup (1 stick) butter
1/2 cup mild ground
  chili pepper
1 tablespoon oregano
1 teaspoon garlic powder
1 teaspoon red pepper

2 teaspoons salt
1 tablespoon paprika
1 (28-ounce) can stewed
  tomatoes
2 (8-ounce) cans tomato sauce
3 (15-ounce) cans light red
  kidney beans
4 cups water

Cook the venison in a large skillet, stirring to break up the meat, until brown and crumbly. Drain in a colander. Sauté the onions and bell peppers in the butter until translucent. Combine all ingredients in a large soup pot. Simmer over low heat for at least 30 minutes. *Makes 12 servings.*

*You can also simmer the chili all day in a large slow cooker. The chili freezes well. Leftovers can be used to top baked potatoes, or layered over mashed potatoes in a baking dish and topped with grated Cheddar cheese. Bake at 375 degrees until heated through.*

# Venison Chili

1 pound lean ground venison
1 (10- to 15-ounce) can stewed
  tomatoes, drained
2 medium onions, chopped
2 tablespoons chili powder
1 (16-ounce) can pinto or
  kidney beans

1 (8-ounce) can tomato sauce
1 (4-ounce) can mushrooms,
  drained, or 8 ounces sliced
  fresh mushrooms
1 tablespoon Worcestershire
  sauce
1 tablespoon soy sauce

Cook the venison in a large skillet, stirring to break up the meat, until brown and crumbly. Combine with the other ingredients in a large pot. Simmer for 1 hour or longer (the longer the better!). *Makes 4 to 6 servings.*

# DEER CHILI

2 pounds ground venison
1 large onion, chopped
1 green bell pepper, chopped
2 (15-ounce) cans chili beans
1 (15-ounce) can tomato sauce
Garlic powder, chili powder,
   cumin and pepper
Water

Cook the meat, onion and bell pepper in a skillet, breaking up the meat, until brown and crumbly. Add the remaining ingredients and enough water to bring to desired consistency. Cook for about 40 minutes. *Makes 8 to 10 servings.*

# VENISON EMPANADA

2 tablespoons vegetable oil,
   divided
1 garlic clove, minced
1 pound chopped venison
1 cup diced onion
1 cup diced potato
1 tablespoon soy sauce
1/4 cup frozen peas
About 4 refrigerated pie pastries
   (or a double-recipe
   homemade pie pastry)

Heat 1 tablespoon of the oil in a skillet over medium heat and sauté the garlic. Add the venison, onion, potato and soy sauce. Cook, breaking up the meat, until the meat is brown and crumbly and the vegetables are softened. Add the peas and heat through. Remove from heat and let cool.

Preheat the oven to 350 degrees. Cut the pastries into 4-inch circles. Gather up and reroll the pastry scraps to cut more circles. Spoon some of the venison mixture on the lower half of the pastry rounds and fold the dough over to enclose. Pinch the edges or press with a fork to seal. Bake until brown or deep-fry in hot oil until brown. Serve hot. *Makes about 16 empanadas.*

# Enchilasagna

2 (10-ounce) cans enchilada sauce
1 (12-ounce) can tomato sauce
1 pound ground venison, cooked and drained
1 tablespoon cumin
1 tablespoon garlic powder
Salt and pepper to taste
12 corn tortillas
1 (15-ounce) can black beans, drained
1 pound reduced-fat Cheddar cheese, shredded

Preheat the oven to 350 degrees and grease a 9x13-inch pan. Combine the enchilada sauce and tomato sauce in a saucepan and bring to a simmer over low heat.

Cook the meat in a skillet, breaking up the chunks, until brown and crumbly. Add the cumin, garlic powder, salt and pepper. Stir half the sauce mixture into the meat and set aside.

Cut each tortilla into 6 pieces.

Pour 3/4 cup of the remaining sauce into the greased pan. Top with 1/3 of the meat, then 1/3 of the beans, then 1/4 of the cheese. Next make a layer of tortillas. Repeat the layers, using all the ingredients and ending with a layer of tortillas, then sauce, then cheese. Bake, uncovered, for 30 to 40 minutes. Let stand for 10 minutes before serving. *Makes 6 servings.*

"I still like to bring home something to grace the dinner
table when I go hunting or fishing, and I can imagine no finer
reason for going. The world was made to be lived in as well as
looked at, and nature's supermarket is well stocked
if you don't mind its self-service feature."
—Havilah Babcock, *The Best of Babcock*

# Pasta e Fagioli

1/2 cup chopped onion
2 garlic cloves, minced
1/2 cup chopped celery
1/2 cup grated carrots
2 tablespoons olive oil
1 (14-ounce) can chicken broth
1/2 pound ground venison
2 (14-ounce) cans diced
  tomatoes
1 (8-ounce) can tomato sauce

1 (16-ounce) can red kidney
  beans, drained
1 (16-ounce) can white kidney
  beans (cannellini), drained
1 cup cooked ditalini, chopped
1/2 teaspoon pepper
1 teaspoon dried parsley
1/2 teaspoon dried basil
1 1/2 teaspoons Italian seasoning
Salt to taste

Sauté the onion, garlic, celery and carrots in the the olive oil in a skillet until tender-crisp. Add the chicken broth and simmer.

Cook the venison in a skillet, breaking up chunks, until brown and crumbly. Add to the vegetables along with the diced tomatoes, tomato sauce and beans. Add the cooked pasta, pepper, parsley, basil, Italian seasoning and salt. Simmer for 20 to 30 minutes. *Makes 4 quarts.*

# Venison Spaghetti

2 tablespoons olive oil
1 to 1 1/2 pounds ground venison
1/2 pound venison sausage
1/2 pound ground beef
1 garlic clove, minced
Dash of pepper, salt and sugar
4 (8-ounce) cans tomato sauce

2 (6-ounce) cans tomato paste
1 onion, chopped
1 green bell pepper, chopped
1 (4-ounce) can chopped
  black olives
1 (4-ounce) can sliced
  mushrooms

Heat the olive oil in a large skillet and brown the meat. Add all the remaining ingredients and mix well. Add about two 8-ounce cans water to thin the mixture. Simmer for 3 hours. Serve over hot cooked noodles with grated Romano cheese. *Makes 8 servings.*

# Spaghetti Sauce and Venison Meatballs

Spaghetti Sauce
3/4 cup chopped onion
2 garlic cloves, minced
1 tablespoon olive oil
1 1/2 cups water
1 (16-ounce) can tomato sauce
1 (12-ounce) can tomato paste
1/4 cup minced fresh parsley
1/2 tablespoon dried basil
1/2 tablespoon dried oregano
1 teaspoon salt
1/4 teaspoon pepper

Venison Meatballs
1 1/2 pounds ground venison
2 eggs, lightly beaten
1 cup soft bread crumbs
3/4 cup milk
1/2 cup grated Parmesan cheese
2 garlic cloves, minced
1 teaspoon salt
1/2 teaspoon pepper
2 tablespoons olive oil

For the sauce, sauté the onion and garlic in the olive oil in a Dutch oven over medium heat. Add the water, tomato sauce, tomato paste, parsley, basil, oregano, salt and pepper. Bring to a boil; reduce heat and simmer, covered, for 1 hour.

For the venison meatballs, combine the ground venison, eggs, bread crumbs, milk, cheese, garlic, salt and pepper in a large bowl and mix well. Shape into 1 1/2-inch balls. Arrange on a baking sheet and refrigerate for several hours or freeze for 15 to 20 minutes. (This chilling is the secret to keeping the meatballs intact as they cook.)

Heat the olive oil in a large skillet over medium heat. Brown the meatballs all over and add to the sauce. Simmer for about 30 minutes, stirring occasionally. Stir gently to avoid damaging the meatballs. Serve over spaghetti. *Makes 6 servings.*

# SPICY VENISON AND BLACK OLIVE ROTINI

2 tablespoons extra-virgin olive oil

1/2 cup chopped onion

2 garlic cloves, minced

1/8 to 1/4 teaspoon red pepper flakes

1/2 pound ground venison

Scant 1/8 teaspoon cinnamon

Kosher salt and freshly ground black pepper to taste

5 ounces rotini

1 (14-ounce) can diced tomatoes

1/4 teaspoon sugar

1/4 cup pitted black olives

1 tablespoon dried parsley

Grated Parmesan cheese

Heat the olive oil in a large skillet over medium heat. Sauté the onion until tender. Add the garlic and red pepper flakes. When the garlic is fragrant but not brown, add the venison and cinnamon. Season generously with salt and black pepper. Cook, breaking up the meat, until brown and crumbly.

Cook the pasta in boiling salted water according to the package directions.

Add the undrained tomatoes to the venison. Reduce heat to medium-low and cook for 8 to 10 minutes. Stir in the sugar, olives and parsley. Taste and add salt and pepper if needed.

Drain the rotini and add to the meat sauce and mix well. Serve immediately and top with additional parsley and Parmesan cheese. *Makes 2 to 3 servings.*

"Among the truly Southern dishes most enjoyed
[at Christmas] are the roasted rice-fed mallards, the venison
sausages, and the crisp, brown corn-breads."
—Archibald Rutledge, *Plantation Game Trails*

# BAKED VENISON ZITI

1 pound ground venison
1/4 to 1/2 pound bulk
  venison sausage
1/2 cup chopped onion
2 garlic cloves, minced
3 1/2 cups meatless
  spaghetti sauce
1 cup chicken broth
1 tablespoon chopped
  fresh oregano

1 tablespoon chopped
  fresh parsley
16 ounces ziti, cooked and
  drained
2 cups shredded mozzarella
  cheese, divided
1 cup grated Parmesan cheese,
  divided

Cook the venison and sausage with the onion and garlic in a large skillet over medium-high heat for 6 to 8 minutes or until the meat is brown and crumbly, stirring to break up the chunks of meat. Stir in the spaghetti sauce, chicken broth, oregano and parsley. Reduce heat and simmer for 10 to 15 minutes. Stir 1 cup of the sauce into the cooked ziti. Spoon half the ziti mixture into a greased 9x13-inch baking dish. Sprinkle with 1 1/2 cups mozzarella and 1/2 cup Parmesan. Top with 2 cups sauce, then the remaining ziti mixture and sauce. Cover and bake in a 350-degree oven for 20 minutes. Sprinkle with the remaining mozzarella and Parmesan. Bake, uncovered, until heated through and cheese is bubbly, about 10 minutes longer. *Makes 8 servings.*

*Try adding 1 cup ricotta cheese in the middle layer with the mozzarella and Parmesan.*

# Hunt Camp Venison Meat Loaf

2 pounds ground venison
1 medium onion, chopped
2 eggs
1 (8-ounce) can tomato sauce
10 (or more) ounces ketchup
2 to 4 tablespoons olive oil, if venison is lean
1/2 cup chopped bell pepper
1 small stalk celery, chopped
1 (4-ounce) can chopped mushrooms, drained
Salt, pepper and Greek seasoning to taste
3 slices bread, toasted and ground into crumbs
Ketchup for glazing

Preheat the oven to 350 degrees. Combine the venison, onion, eggs, tomato sauce, 10 ounces ketchup, olive oil, bell pepper, celery, mushrooms, salt, pepper and Greek seasoning in a large bowl and mix well. Add bread crumbs to the mixture until it is stiff enough to form a loaf. Shape into 1 large or 2 small loaves in a roasting or other pan. Spread with ketchup. Bake for 45 minutes (for small loaves) to 1 hour. *Makes 6 to 8 servings.*

# Tamale Pie

1 1/2 to 2 pounds ground venison
1/2 to 1 envelope taco seasoning
1 (8-ounce) can tomato sauce
Sautéed chopped onion, hot chili powder, diced green chiles or chopped fresh jalapeño pepper (optional)
1 package small flour tortillas
1 or 2 (4-ounce) cans sliced black olives
1 (8-ounce) package shredded Cheddar cheese
1 (8-ounce) package shredded Monterey Jack or mozzarella

Cook the meat in a skillet, breaking up chunks, until brown and crumbly. Add the taco seasoning mix and tomato sauce and any of the optional ingredients. Preheat the oven to 350 degrees. Place a tortilla in the bottom of a round baking dish. Spread with some of the meat, olives and cheese. Repeat the layering, ending with cheese. Bake for 30 minutes or until heated through and cheese is bubbling. *Makes 4 to 6 servings.*

# BURGERS WITH BALSAMIC CARAMELIZED ONION

**BALSAMIC CARAMELIZED ONION**
1 tablespoon olive oil
1 large onion, sliced
1 teaspoon sugar
1/4 to 1/2 teaspoon balsamic
   vinegar
1/4 teaspoon kosher salt

**BURGERS**
1 pound ground venison
1 tablespoon dried parsley, or
   1/4 cup chopped fresh parsley
2 tablespoons tomato paste
1 teaspoon steak seasoning
1/2 teaspoon kosher salt
1/4 teaspoon freshly ground
   pepper
1 1/2 teaspoons olive oil

For the onion, heat the olive oil in a large nonstick skillet and cook the onion and sugar over low heat for 20 to 25 minutes or until the onion is caramel-colored, stirring frequently. Stir in the vinegar and salt. Set the mixture aside and keep warm.

For the burgers, combine the ground venison, parsley, tomato paste, steak seasoning, salt and pepper in a bowl and shape into 4 patties. Brush with the olive oil. Grill in a covered pan over medium-high heat for 5 minutes per side or to desired doneness. Serve open-faced on grilled garlic Texas toast with caramelized onion, sliced tomatoes and basil mayonnaise. *Makes 4 servings.*

# SPICY MEAT SANDWICHES

1 pound ground venison
1 pound bulk pork sausage
1 pound Velveeta
3/4 teaspoon oregano

Dash of garlic powder
Dash of Tabasco sauce
1 to 1 1/2 loaves party rye bread

Cook the venison and pork in a large skillet, breaking up the chunks, until brown and crumbly. Drain. Stir in the process cheese and cook over low heat until the cheese is melted. Add the oregano, garlic powder and Tabasco sauce and mix well. Spread the mixture over the rye bread.

Flash-freeze the sandwiches for 10 to 15 minutes, then pack into heavy plastic zip-top bags and freeze until ready to serve. Bake at 400 degrees until hot and bubbly, about 5 to 8 minutes. *Makes 15 to 20 sandwiches.*

# MEATBALLS IN CURRANT SAUCE

1 1/2 pounds ground venison
1/2 cup dry bread crumbs
1/2 cup milk
1 egg, beaten
1/4 cup minced onion
1 1/2 teaspoons salt

1/4 teaspoon pepper
1/4 teaspoon garlic powder, or
1 fresh garlic clove, minced
1 (10-ounce) jar red currant
jelly
1 (12-ounce) jar chili sauce

Preheat the oven to 350 degrees. Combine the venison, bread crumbs, milk, egg, onion, salt, pepper and garlic powder in a bowl and mix well. Shape into 1-inch balls. Arrange in a baking dish and bake for about 30 minutes or until browned. Drain if needed.

Heat the red currant jelly and chili sauce in a large skillet, stirring until well combined. Add the meatballs and simmer for 30 minutes. Serve hot in a chafing dish. *Makes about 25 meatballs.*

# Venison Neck Jerky

Cut the deer neck off where it attaches to the skull and again just forward of the shoulder. Trim the extraneous membranes and wipe dry. Refrigerate until thoroughly chilled. Cut the meat from the bone in quarter sections and flatten on a cutting board. Cut with the grain of the meat into long strips. Combine the meat and teriyaki or soy sauce in a large zip-top bag. Press all of the air out of the bag. Refrigerate for 8 hours or more.

Working in batches, arrange the meat close together in rows on a rack and put the rack in a roasting pan. Sprinkle with black pepper and salt. Set the oven to the lowest possible heat and place the pan in the middle of the oven until the meat is fairly stiff, an hour or more.

Repeat the process to dry all of the meat. Pack the dried strips in a zip-top bag and store in the freezer.

"After a day-long tramp behind a brace of ambitious
dogs a man doesn't need an appetizer when he sits down
to dinner, nor a lullaby when he goes to bed."
—Havilah Babcock, *The Best of Babcock*

WILD FARE &
WISE WORDS

# WATERFOWL

# WATERFOWL

A posthumously published book written by Nash Buckingham
is entitled *Once Upon a Time.* In that work, as is the case in much of his writing,
he looks longingly back to the days "when ducks were plenty."
In one particularly poignant piece, "The Prodigal Years," he even accepts
his small part of the blame for having bagged fifty ducks a day
(a limit at his beloved Beaver Dam Club, not the law) time and again.
That was an era when punt guns ruled supreme, when waterfowl figured
prominently on the menus of fine restaurants, and when untold barrels
of salted ducks were shipped from the Mississippi flyway to cities
along the Eastern seaboard.

The day of the market hunters who called Chesapeake Bay and
Louisiana bayous home has long passed, and even the advent of
strict limits, federal regulations, and a waterfowl stamp was in
large degree a case of too little, too late. Thankfully though, we still
have the opportunity to sit, shivering deliciously, while awaiting
a January dawn at the arrival of legal shooting hours.
Whistling wings echoing through the mist still have their special thrill,
and at least there are enough ducks for the hunter to entertain
fond hopes of a special meal.

# Roasted Wild Duck with Stuffing

1 wild duck, dressed
1 teaspoon each salt, oregano
  and paprika
1/2 teaspoon pepper
1/4 cup olive oil
1/4 cup lemon juice
1 (14-ounce) can chicken broth

1 package Knorr vegetable
  soup mix
6 tablespoons butter
3 celery stalks, chopped
1 onion, chopped
4 cups herb-seasoned
  stuffing mix

Preheat the oven to 350 degrees. Place the duck on a rack in a roasting pan. Combine the salt, oregano, paprika, pepper, oil and lemon juice and use the mixture to coat the duck. Bake, covered, for 1 1/2 hours. Uncover and bake for 30 minutes longer.

Combine the broth and soup mix in a small saucepan. Bring to a boil and simmer for 5 minutes.

Melt the butter in a skillet and sauté the celery and onion until tender. Combine the stuffing mix, broth mixture and celery and onion in a large serving bowl. Serve with the duck. *Makes 1 to 2 servings.*


# Barbecued Duck

2 wild ducks, cut into halves
1 cup ketchup
1/2 cup lemon juice
1 tablespoon Worcestershire
  sauce

1/4 cup packed brown sugar
1/2 teaspoon each salt, black
  pepper and paprika
1 teaspoon hot red pepper sauce

Preheat the oven to 325 degrees. Arrange the duck halves on a rack in a roasting pan. Combine the remaining ingredients in a saucepan. Bring to a low boil and simmer for about 5 minutes. Spread some of the sauce on the duck and cover with foil. Bake for 1 1/2 hours. Remove the foil and spoon on the remaining sauce. Increase the heat to 375 degrees and bake, uncovered, for 20 minutes longer. *Makes 4 to 6 servings.*

# European Wild Duck

1 (16-ounce) bottle olive oil and
   vinegar salad dressing
4 boneless wild duck breasts
1 (15-ounce) container ricotta
   cheese
1 package Knorr vegetable
   soup mix

2 (10-ounce) packages frozen
   spinach, thawed, drained and
   squeezed dry
1 ounce feta cheese, crumbled
1 tablespoon butter
3/4 cup slivered almonds

Reserve 1/4 cup of the salad dressing. Marinate the duck in the remaining salad dressing in the refrigerator for at least 2 hours.

Preheat the oven to 325 degrees. Combine the ricotta cheese and soup mix in a bowl. Add the spinach and mix well. Spread the mixture in an 8-inch square baking dish. Arrange the duck on top of the ricotta mixture. Combine the feta cheese with the reserved dressing. Spread the mixture over the duck. Bake for 1 hour and 15 minutes.

Melt the butter in a skillet and sauté the almonds until golden. Sprinkle over the duck and serve. *Makes 4 servings.*

# Duck Kabobs

2 puddle ducks (mallard, wood
   duck, teal)
Cayenne pepper (optional)

1 pound bacon
Barbecue sauce

Fillet the breast meat from the ducks. Cut the fillets lengthwise once, then cut crosswise to make cubes of approximately 1 inch. For spicy kabobs, dust the meat with cayenne. Cut the bacon into slices just long enough to wrap around each duck cube. Skewer with a wooden pick to hold the bacon in place. Dip each piece into barbecue sauce and grill until the bacon is cooked through. Serve as an appetizer.

*Soaking the wooden picks in water for about 30 minutes prior to grilling will prevent burning.*

# POT-ROASTED WILD DUCK

2 to 4 wild ducks, cleaned,
   skin on
Salt and pepper to taste
1 white onion, diced
3 celery stalks, diced
1 bell pepper, diced
1 tablespoon minced garlic
2 tablespoons mustard
1 (16-ounce) bottle Italian
   salad dressing

1/4 cup vegetable oil
1/2 cup (1 stick) butter
2 teaspoons salt
1 teaspoon Cajun seasoning
5 cups water
1 bunch green onions, chopped
1 bunch parsley, chopped

Rub the ducks with salt and pepper and cut slits in both sides of the breast. Combine the onion, celery, bell pepper, garlic and mustard and stuff into the slits. Place the ducks in a large bowl and cover with Italian dressing. Marinate in the refrigerator.

Heat the oil in a Dutch oven and brown the ducks. Heat the butter in a skillet and sauté the onion, celery, bell pepper, garlic, 2 teaspoons salt, Cajun seasoning and the marinade until the vegetables are tender. Add to the ducks along with the water. Bring to a boil, then simmer for 15 minutes.

Preheat the oven to 350 degrees. Cover the Dutch oven and bake for 1 1/2 to 2 hours, stirring every 30 minutes. Check the liquid and add more if needed. After 1 hour, add the green onions and parsley to the Dutch oven. Serve the meat with hot cooked rice, corn bread and lima beans or stewed potatoes. *Makes 4 to 6 servings.*

# DUCK BREAST SUPREME

4 whole mallards, dressed
1 cup all-purpose flour
1 teaspoon salt
Pepper to taste
$^{1}/_{2}$ teaspoon garlic powder, or 1 teaspoon Cajun seasoning
3 to 4 tablespoons vegetable oil or olive oil
2 to 3 tablespoons butter or margarine
2 small onions
1 cup white wine
Lemon juice (optional)

Split the ducks into halves and lay flat. Combine the flour with salt, pepper and garlic powder. Coat the duck pieces with the flour mixture, shaking off the excess. Heat the oil in a saucepan with the butter and brown the duck pieces. Preheat the oven to 350 degrees.

Arrange the meat in a baking dish. Cut the onions into halves and place an onion half in each corner. Pour the wine into the dish. Cover and bake for 1 hour. Remove the cover during the last 10 to 15 minutes and spoon the pan juices over the meat. To serve, squeeze a few drops of lemon juice over the duck. *Makes 4 servings.*

"To many people a taste of duck is a rare treat, and a
supper of properly cooked duck, with acceptable trimmings,
is a notable dispenser of pleasure and happiness."
—Harry Hampton, *Woods and Waters and Some Asides*

# BAKED DUCK BREASTS

DUCK BREASTS
4 filleted duck breasts
12 tablespoons (1 1/2 sticks)
  butter (no substitute),
  chopped
4 bay leaves
1 tablespoon poultry seasoning
1 tablespoon dried chives, or
  3 tablespoons fresh chives
1 tablespoon parsley flakes

1/2 teaspoon garlic salt
Dash of cinnamon
Pepper to taste

ORANGE SAUCE
1/4 cup sugar
1 teaspoon nutmeg
1 tablespoon cornstarch
1 cup orange juice

For the duck breasts, preheat the oven to 350 degrees. Place the duck breasts on a sheet of aluminum foil large enough to enclose and seal. Dot the duck with bits of butter and place a bay leaf on each fillet. Sprinkle the remaining seasonings over the duck. Fold the foil to enclose the duck and seal. Bake until tender, about 1 hour and 15 minutes.

For the sauce, combine the sugar, nutmeg and cornstarch in a medium saucepan. Stir in a little orange juice and mix well, then add the remaining orange juice. Cook the mixture, stirring, over medium heat until it boils and thickens.

Remove the duck breasts from the oven and unwrap. Discard the bay leaves. Serve with the orange sauce. *Makes 4 servings.*

*The orange sauce is also good served with goose, turkey, game birds and venison.*

"With the dedicated hunter, the sport is in his blood. It is said that one celebrated Nimrod went duck hunting, when weather conditions came right, while his mother was lying in state."
—Harry Hampton, *Woods and Waters and Some Asides*

# Duck Bog

2 (10-ounce) cans chicken broth
2 large onions, cut into quarters
Salt and pepper to taste
3 or 4 ducks
1 pound bulk pork sausage
1 pound smoked link sausage, chopped
1 large onion, diced
1 bell pepper, any color
4 ounces sliced mushrooms
1 (10-ounce) can French onion soup
3 cups uncooked rice

Combine the chicken broth and onions in a heavy pot large enough to hold the ducks. Season with salt and pepper and add the ducks, plus enough water to cover. Bring to a boil, reduce heat, and simmer for 1 1/2 to 2 hours.

Heat a large skillet and sauté the bulk sausage, link sausage, onion and bell pepper. Break up the bulk sausage and cook until the vegetables are tender. Drain. Cool the ducks and tear the meat into bite-sized pieces.

Measure 5 cups of the duck broth into a large saucepan or Dutch oven. Bring to a simmer and add the ducks, sausage mixture, mushrooms and rice and mix well. Reduce the heat to low, cover, and simmer until the rice is tender, about 20 minutes. (Or combine the ingredients in a large roasting pan and bake, covered, at 350 degrees until the rice is tender.)

# Cajun Duck Hors d'Oeuvre

8 to 10 wild mallard duck
   breast halves
1/2 pound green chile peppers

1 pound sliced bacon
1 bottle Allegro marinade or
   Dale's seasoning

Cut the duck breasts into 3/4- to 1-inch-wide strips across the grain of the meat. If pieces are very thick, cut into halves. Cut the peppers lengthwise into halves or thirds, discarding the ribs and seeds. Cut the bacon slices into halves. Roll a piece of duck around a slice of pepper, then wrap with bacon and secure with a wooden pick. Arrange the pieces in a glass dish and pour the marinade over them. Refrigerate for at least 1 hour and up to 12. Prepare a gas grill or charcoal fire. Grill the pieces, turning occasionally, until the bacon is crisp. Do not overcook.

# Duck Jerky

Duck meat
1 cup soy sauce
1/4 cup Worcestershire sauce

1/4 cup liquid smoke
Garlic pepper

Cut duck meat crosswise into 1/8-inch-thick pieces. For chewier jerky, slice the meat lengthwise along the breast.

Combine the soy sauce, Worcestershire sauce and liquid smoke in a glass dish or zip-top bag. Add the duck and marinate in the refrigerator for 8 to 12 hours.

Arrange the meat on a dehydrator and sprinkle with garlic pepper. Dehydrate until desired dryness is reached. Store in an airtight container, or for longer-term, store in the freezer.

# Sesame Goose

GOOSE
1 pound goose breasts
1$^{1}/_{2}$ tablespoons rice wine
1 teaspoon sugar
1 tablespoon grated ginger
1$^{1}/_{2}$ tablespoons cornstarch
1$^{1}/_{2}$ tablespoons sesame oil
1 tablespoon soy sauce
Vegetable oil for frying

SAUCE
2 tablespoons hoisin sauce
1 tablespoon Thai chili sauce
$^{1}/_{2}$ tablespoon sugar
2 tablespoons water
1 tablespoon sesame oil
1 garlic clove, crushed
1 teaspoon vegetable oil
1 teaspoon toasted sesame seeds
1 teaspoon sesame oil

Place the meat in the freezer for 30 minutes to make it easier to slice thinly. Cut into thin slices across the grain.

Combine the wine, sugar, ginger, cornstarch, sesame oil and soy sauce in a large bowl. Add the goose slices and refrigerate for 1 hour.

Heat vegetable oil in a large skillet and fry the slices until slightly crisp. Drain on paper towels.

Combine the hoisin sauce, chili sauce, sugar, water and 1 tablespoon sesame oil in a small bowl. Heat the vegetable oil in a large skillet and sauté the garlic clove until fragrant. Pour in the hoisin mixture and cook, stirring, until thickened.

Add the goose to the sauce and cook, stirring, until heated through. Garnish with the sesame seeds and 1 teaspoon sesame oil. Serve with hot cooked rice.

*This treatment works equally well with venison.*

WILD FARE &
WISE WORDS

# WILD
# TURKEY

# WILD TURKEY

Thanks to its association with the first Thanksgiving, early in the seventeenth century, the American wild turkey has long held a proud place in our nation's culinary history. Pilgrims and Native Americans dined on the big bird because it was plentiful and delicious. Today, thanks to what ranks as one of the greatest wildlife comeback sagas, the ever-growing ranks of those who hunt turkeys can make a meaningful connection with this chapter from the past.

The wild turkey is a far cry from its overweight, awkward domestic cousin in appearance and agility. Also, while barnyard turkeys are literally so dumb they sometimes drown themselves while looking up into pouring rain, such is definitely not the case with the wily, "wired" creature now found in every state but Alaska. They also bring distinctly different qualities to the table. While I would not for a moment deny the gustatory pleasures to be derived from a carefully basted and perfectly browned "Butterball," by preference I'll opt for a wild bird.

Treat wild turkeys with special care, for they are truly special. That means dressing them in the field so the body cavity will cool rapidly (carry a zip-top bag to store the heart, liver, and gizzard if you want to save the giblets), plucking rather than skinning them for maximum moistness, and cooking them in proper fashion. The recipes that follow give you plenty of options to do just that, even as they guarantee feasts that the Pilgrims would have envied.

# Brined Wild Turkey

1¹/₄ cups kosher salt  
1 gallon water  
1 wild turkey, cleaned  
2 Granny Smith apples  

1 large onion  
3 celery stalks  
Freshly ground pepper  
  to taste  

Dissolve the salt in the water in a container large enough to hold the turkey (or a roasting bag or clean plastic trash bag). Lower the turkey into the water. Refrigerate for 8 to 12 hours or store in an ice chest surrounded by ice.

Preheat the oven to 400 degrees. Remove the turkey from the brine and discard the brine. Rinse the turkey and pat dry. Cut the apples and onions into slices and the celery into 3-inch pieces. Place these in the cavity of the turkey and on and around it. Season the turkey with pepper. Arrange in a large roasting pan.

Roast, breast side up, for 30 minutes. Lower the heat to 325 degrees, turn the turkey breast side down and bake for 1¹/₂ hours. Turn again and bake until cooked through, about 25 minutes per pound. Let stand until slightly cooled before carving. *Makes 10 servings.*

*Use apples, cut into wedges, to brace the turkey when it is roasting breast side down.*

# Three-Minute Fried Turkey

1 wild turkey breast fillet  
2 cups milk  
1 cup self-rising flour  

1 teaspoon salt  
¹/₄ teaspoon pepper  
1 gallon cooking oil  

Cut the meat across the grain into finger-size strips. Soak in milk for at least 1 hour and up to 12. Combine the flour, salt and pepper in a bag or on a plate. Drain the meat and coat with the flour mixture. Heat 1 gallon oil to 350 degrees in a deep fat fryer. Cook the turkey for 3 minutes, then drain on paper towels. Don't overcook or the meat will be dry and tough. *Makes 8 to 10 servings.*

# FRIED WILD TURKEY BREAST

1 wild turkey breast
  (2 breast halves)
2 cups buttermilk
2 cups flour

Salt and pepper to taste
1 1/2 to 2 cups vegetable oil
1 cup milk
1 cup water

Cut the turkey across the grain into 1/2-inch slices. Cover with buttermilk and refrigerate for 30 minutes or more. Combine the flour with salt and pepper and coat the turkey with the mixture. Heat the oil in a large skillet and fry the turkey until brown. Turn the pieces, cover the skillet and let cook for a few minutes longer. Remove the lid and continue cooking until pieces no longer stick to the bottom. Drain on paper towels.

Drain all but 1/4 cup oil from the skillet. Sift 3 to 4 tablespoons of the flour mixture over the oil. Cook, stirring, until brown. Add the milk and water to the skillet and mix well. Cook, stirring constantly, until thickened. If gravy becomes too thick, add more water. Serve with turkey.
*Makes 8 to 10 servings.*

# DEEP-FRIED TURKEY

3 to 5 gallons peanut oil for
  deep-frying
1 wild turkey, cleaned
Seasonings of choice

Liquid seasonings to inject, such
  as hot pepper sauce, Italian
  salad dressing, liquid Cajun
  seasoning

Heat the oil to 300 to 350 degrees. Rub the turkey with seasonings and inject with further seasonings, if desired. Hook a wire coathanger around each of the drumsticks and carefully lower the turkey into the oil. Cook for 3 1/2 to 4 1/2 minutes per pound or until a meat thermometer inserted into the white meat registers 180 degrees. The turkey tends to float when cooked through. Remove the turkey from the oil and drain well. Wrap in foil to keep warm. Let stand for 15 to 20 minutes before carving. *Makes 10 servings.*

# Black Walnut–Crusted Turkey

1 pound wild turkey breast cutlets
1/2 cup oil and vinegar salad dressing
1/3 cup finely chopped black walnuts
1/2 cup fresh bread crumbs
1 tablespoon finely chopped fresh chives
1 tablespoon margarine
2 tablespoons olive oil

Pound the cutlets with a meat mallet to a uniform thickness. Combine with the salad dressing in a plastic zip-top bag. Refrigerate for 6 to 8 hours.

Process the walnuts and bread crumbs in a food processor until finely chopped. Add the chives and pulse to blend.

Heat the margarine and olive oil in a large skillet over medium-high heat. Drain the cutlets and coat with the walnut mixture, pressing the mixture into the cutlets so it will adhere. Place the turkey in the skillet and lower the heat to medium. Cook until golden brown outside and no longer pink inside, about 4 to 6 minutes per side. Serve immediately. *Makes 4 servings.*

# Turkey "Leg Fingers"

2 whole turkey legs
Salt and pepper to taste
1 1/2 cups self-rising flour or biscuit mix
1 cup milk
1 tablespoon butter or margarine
2 tablespoons vegetable oil or shortening

Boil the turkey in water to cover until tender. Let cool, then slice the meat into 1-inch strips. Season with salt and pepper. Combine the flour, milk and butter to make a stiff batter. Dip the meat strips into the batter.

Heat the oil in a skillet and fry the strips, turning once. Drain on paper towels. *Makes 4 servings.*

*Too many hunters discard the tough-but-meaty wild turkey legs. Using a pressure cooker cuts the boiling time in half. The leg meat can also be ground, then formed into patties or meat loaf.*

# Turkey Scallopini with Asparagus Sauce

1 envelope béarnaise sauce mix
3 tablespoons cooked
    chopped leeks
1 (15-ounce) can asparagus
    spears, chopped
1 pound wild turkey breast fillets

2 tablespoons butter
2 tablespoons olive oil
1/2 cup all-purpose flour
1/2 to 1 cup grated
    Parmesan cheese

Prepare the béarnaise sauce according to the package directions. Warm the leeks in the microwave. Add the leeks and half the asparagus to the sauce and set aside.

Pound the turkey fillets with a meat mallet to tenderize. Melt the butter in a skillet and add the olive oil. Lightly coat the breast fillets with flour and cook on each side until golden brown. Place the turkey in a greased shallow 9x13-inch baking dish. Spread the asparagus sauce over the turkey. Sprinkle with the cheese and broil to brown the cheese. Serve at once. Serve with wild rice and squash medley. *Makes 6 servings.*

*Wild turkey will never be as tender as chicken, but pounding with a meat mallet helps a great deal. This dish is best served right away and doesn't reheat well.*

"Here the Christmas breakfaster may regale himself
on plantation fare: snowy hominy, cold wild turkey, brown
crumbly corn-breads, venison sausages, beaten biscuits,
steaming coffee, home-made orange marmalade."
—Archibald Rutledge, *My Colonel and His Lady*

# BEAGLE CLUB PIE

1 1/2 to 2 pounds wild turkey
    breast fillets
1 1/2 to 2 quarts chicken broth
Salt and pepper to taste
3 hard-boiled eggs

1 (10-ounce) can cream of
    chicken soup
1 cup biscuit mix
1 cup whole milk

Cook the turkey breast in the chicken broth until tender; reserve the broth. Cut the meat into bite-size pieces and arrange in a 12-inch square baking dish. Season with salt and pepper. Slice the eggs over the meat. Combine the soup with an equal amount of broth and pour over the meat. Refrigerate the mixture for at least 2 hours to allow it to firm up.

Preheat the oven to 375 degrees. Combine the biscuit mix and milk and pour over the mixture. Bake, uncovered, until the topping is brown, about 1 hour. Serve hot. *Makes 6 servings.*

*This recipe works equally well with two pheasants.*

# SPINACH STRAWBERRY TURKEY SALAD

2 tablespoons strawberry jam
2 tablespoons white cider
    vinegar
1/3 cup canola oil
8 cups torn fresh spinach

1 cup sliced fresh strawberries
2 cups chopped cooked
    wild turkey
1 cup seedless grape halves
1/2 cup toasted slivered almonds

Combine the jam and vinegar in a blender container and process until blended. With the motor on, add the oil gradually.

Combine the spinach, strawberries, turkey and grapes in a large bowl and mix well. Pour the dressing over the salad and toss to coat. Top with almonds. Serve immediately. *Makes 8 servings.*

# Turkey and Wild Rice Soup

6 tablespoons margarine
1/2 cup chopped onion
1 cup chopped celery
1/2 cup chopped carrots
1/2 cup sliced fresh mushrooms
6 tablespoons all-purpose flour

Salt and pepper to taste
2 (10-ounce) cans chicken broth
4 cups milk
2 cups cooked wild rice
2 cups cubed cooked turkey

Melt the margarine in a large pan and sauté the onion, celery, carrots and mushrooms until tender-crisp. Stir in the flour, salt and pepper and mix well.

Add the chicken broth and milk and cook, stirring, until thickened. Add the wild rice and turkey. Adjust seasonings. Simmer until heated through. *Makes 8 servings.*

*Dark meat adds a lot to the flavor of the soup, so try to use
a combination of dark and white meat.*

"In state we hung up the Gunner's buck, and then
went in to a wild turkey dinner and an hour of perfect
peace, yarning before the great open fireside."
—Archibald Rutledge, *An American Hunter* (1937)

WILD FARE &
WISE WORDS

# UPLAND
# GAME BIRDS

# UPLAND GAME BIRDS

Hunting birds is one of America's most cherished sporting traditions. We cling to the image of a stylish pointer frozen against an evening sky while holding tight on a sunset covey close to a corner of our sporting souls. For many of the men whose quotations add spice to this book, hunting upland birds was a lifelong pilgrimage of passion. It furnished the primary subject material for Robert Ruark, Havilah Babcock, and Nash Buckingham, and few "all-purpose outdoor writers," sort of the literary equivalent of what old-timers describe as "an all-around meat dog," overlook the appeal of flying feathers in their scattergun sketches. Less likely to produce flights of literary fancy, but nonetheless important to any meaningful understanding of the totality of American hunting, are outings for squirrels and rabbits, 'possums and 'coons.

For some reason, though, upland birds tend to be neglected in many game cookbooks. Maybe because it takes a lot to make a little, or as my grandfather used to say about doves, "You get a lot of gravy for a little meat." Yet when properly prepared, there are few things more delectable or delightful than upland game birds and animals. Grandpa Joe was of the fixed opinion that "there's nothing finer than properly cooked pottiges" (a generic term commonly used throughout the South to describe birds— and for the uninitiated "bird" means quail). Nor should the fact that no matter where you live, in all likelihood you have ready access to one or more species of upland game birds. The recipes that follow remind us of the fine and varied fare that comes from such hunting.

# GRILLED DOVE

12 dove breasts  
Seasoned salt (such as Lawry's)

1 pound bacon, slices cut into  
halves crosswise

Thoroughly wash the dove breasts. Sprinkle liberally with seasoned salt. Wrap a half-slice of bacon around each dove breast and secure with a wooden pick. Place on a hot charcoal grill with the flat side of the dove breast down. Grill for 25 to 30 minutes, turning occasionally. *Makes 3 servings.*

# DOVES BURGUNDY

1/2 cup (1 stick) butter  
3 tablespoons minced onion  
1 1/2 cups burgundy

12 dove breasts  
3 tablespoons all-purpose flour  
1/4 cup cold water

Melt the butter in a cast-iron Dutch oven or heavy pot with a lid; add the onion, wine and dove breasts, bone-side down. Cover and cook over low heat until the meat is tender. Remove the meat from the liquid. Dissolve the flour in the cold water. Bring the wine mixture to a boil. Add the flour mixture, and cook, whisking until the liquid thickens into a gravy.

Serve with mashed potatoes and lima beans. Spoon the gravy over the potatoes; will make a small puppy pull a large freight train! *Makes 4 servings.*

# BAKED DOVES

8 slices bacon  
8 dove breasts

1 onion, sliced  
1 cup white wine

Preheat the oven to 350 degrees. Wrap a slice of bacon around each dove breast. Place in a baking dish, meaty side down. Cover with sliced onion. Pour the wine over the dove. Bake for 1 hour. *Makes 4 servings.*

# Dove Appetizers

Dove breasts
Vinaigrette or Italian
   salad dressing

Bacon slices, cut into halves and
   precooked a bit in the
   microwave

Marinate dove breasts in your favorite oil and vinegar dressing in the refrigerator for at least 4 hours. Wrap a slice of bacon around each dove breast and secure with a wooden pick. Place on a hot grill and cook for approximately 8 to 10 minutes, turning often, until the center is pink.

*Wrap each dove breast around a jalapeño pepper half and an onion slice, or a water chestnut, or pepper cheese before wrapping with bacon.*

# Dove Purlieu

2 limits of dove breast (24)
1 pound smoked sausage or
   encased venison sausage
1 large onion, diced

3 to 4 tablespoons butter
2 cups (1 pound) white rice
1 (8-ounce) can mushrooms
Salt and pepper to taste

Cook the dove breasts in enough water to cover all 24 of them in a large pot until the meat separates easily from the bones. Remove the meat and keep it at hand. Remove bones and shot from the liquid. Reserve enough of the liquid to cook the rice. Cut the sausage into small pieces and cook briefly in the liquid until they begin to swell. If you use encased venison sausage, brown the entire sausage in the oven, then cut it into small pieces and add to the liquid. Sauté the onion in the butter in a skillet until tender. Add the rice, dove, onion, mushrooms, salt and pepper to the pot and bring the liquid back to a boil. Reduce heat and cook according to the rice package directions. *Makes 6 servings.*

*This works very well with duck breasts also, especially small ducks such as teal and woodies.*

# "Birdy" Dirty Rice

1 cup uncooked long grain
  white rice
2¹/2 cups chicken stock or broth,
  divided
4 tablespoons (¹/2 stick) butter
8 ounces dove breasts (8 to 12),
  coarsely chopped

1 cup finely chopped onion
¹/2 cup finely chopped celery
2 garlic cloves, finely chopped
¹/2 teaspoon black pepper
¹/2 teaspoon cayenne pepper
Chopped green onions

Cook the rice in 2 cups chicken stock for about 20 minutes. Heat the butter in a large skillet and fry the dove until the pink color is gone. Add the onion, celery, garlic, black pepper and cayenne pepper. Sauté for 5 minutes or until the vegetables are softened. Add ¹/2 cup chicken stock and the cooked rice. Cover and simmer over low heat until the liquid is absorbed. Garnish with chopped green onions and serve with hot sauce. *Makes 4 servings.*

# Grilled Quail

6 to 8 dressed quail
1 cup orange juice
1 cup white wine
¹/2 cup olive oil

1 garlic clove
¹/4 teaspoon salt
¹/4 teaspoon pepper
Rosemary

Combine the quail, orange juice, wine, olive oil, garlic, salt, pepper and rosemary in a bowl or plastic zip-top bag. Marinate in the refrigerator for 2 hours. Heat the grill to hot. Drain the quail and grill for 3 minutes on each side. Do not overcook. Serve on green salad with balsamic vinaigrette dressing. *Makes 3 to 4 servings.*

# Smothered Quail

6 whole quail
1/2 cup (1 stick) butter
1/4 cup olive oil

2 (10-ounce) cans chicken with
 rice soup
1/2 cup sherry

Preheat the oven to 350 degrees. Brown the quail in a mixture of butter and olive oil in a skillet. Arrange the quail in a baking dish. Pour the soup and sherry into the pan drippings in the skillet. Bring to a boil and pour over the quail. Cover and bake for 1 hour. Serve with rice and curried fruit. *Makes 4 to 6 servings.*

# Marinated Grilled Quail

Combine equal parts bourbon and apricot jam, seasoning with salt and pepper. Split the quail down the back and soak in the marinade in the refrigerator for 3 to 4 hours. Prepare a charcoal fire. Grill the quail, inside downward, until well browned. Turn and grill the other side.

*Don't forget to use a little of that bourbon on the cook. It's essential to outdoor cooking that the cook must occasionally be basted, but take care that the cook doesn't become marinated.*

# Fried Quail

1 cup red wine
1 cup olive oil
1 tablespoon minced garlic
16 dressed quail

3 cups self-rising flour
1/4 cup seasoned salt
Vegetable oil for deep-frying

Mix the red wine, olive oil and garlic. Add the quail and marinate, refrigerated, for 4 to 6 hours. Combine the flour and seasoned salt. Coat the quail in the mixture and deep-fry in 350-degree oil for 15 to 20 minutes. Serve immediately. *Makes 8 servings.*

# GAME BIRD CHOWDER

1 onion, chopped
1 green bell pepper, chopped
Bacon drippings
1 1/2 pounds red potatoes, skin on, cut into bite-size pieces
3 cups cooked game bird meat (dove, quail, chukkar, pheasant)
2 cups game bird stock or chicken stock
1 quart milk
1 1/2 to 2 cups heavy cream or half-and-half
Salt and pepper to taste
1 teaspoon hot red pepper sauce
10 to 12 slices bacon, cooked and crumbled
Chives (optional)

Sauté the onion and bell pepper in bacon drippings until tender. Add the potatoes and cook until they are fork-tender, about 10 to 15 minutes. Add the meat and stock and simmer for 10 minutes.

Add the milk and cream at serving time and heat over low heat; do not boil. (Add cornstarch or cracker crumbs for a thicker soup.) Season with salt, pepper and hot pepper sauce. Top with crumbled bacon and chives. Serve with hot pepper sauce. *Makes 4 to 6 servings.*

"Any birds?" "Yes, I brought back some and left some,
and it is possible that those I left gave me as much pleasure as
those I brought home. There is only one thing you can
do with a dead bird, you know—eat it."
—Havilah Babcock, *The Best of Babcock*

# GAME POTPIE

4 tablespoons butter  
1 pound cooked game bird meat  
1 cup sliced fresh mushrooms  
2 to 3 tablespoons  
    all-purpose flour  
1/4 teaspoon each salt and pepper  

2 tablespoons dried parsley  
2/3 cup half-and-half  
1 cup sautéed carrots  
1 cup frozen peas  
Pastry dough for a 2-crust  
    deep-dish pie  

Preheat the oven to 400 degrees. Melt 1 tablespoon butter in a skillet and sauté the meat; set aside. Heat 2 tablespoons butter and sauté the mushrooms until tender. Set aside with the meat. Melt the remaining 1 tablespoon butter and add the flour, stirring until smooth. Add the salt, pepper and parsley, then stir in the half-and-half. Bring to a boil and add the carrots, peas, meat and mushrooms. Let cool. Press the pastry into a 2-quart casserole and spoon in the meat mixture. Roll out the remaining dough and top the pie, trimming the edge and pressing to seal. Bake for 30 minutes or until golden brown and heated through. *Makes 4 to 6 servings.*

# PAN-FRIED PHEASANT BREAST

4 to 6 boneless pheasant breasts  
1 1/2 to 2 cups self-rising flour,  
    seasoned with salt and pepper  
2 eggs, beaten  
1 cup seasoned bread crumbs  
1/4 cup olive oil  

1/4 cup (1/2 stick) butter  
1/4 cup white wine  
1/2 cup heavy cream  
1 teaspoon sugar  
Salt and pepper to taste  

Pound the meat with a mallet to 1/4-inch thickness. Coat the meat with the flour, dip in the eggs, then coat with bread crumbs. Heat the oil and butter in a large skillet and fry the meat for 3 to 4 minutes per side or until brown on each side. Remove and keep warm. Pour the wine into the skillet and stir to loosen the brown bits. Add the cream and sugar and cook until thick. Season to taste and spoon over the pheasant. *Makes 4 servings.*

# Pheasant Paprikash

2 tablespoons canola oil
1 large onion, chopped
1 large green bell pepper, sliced (optional)
1 teaspoon paprika, or to taste
1 large fresh tomato, or 1 (15-ounce) can tomatoes
Few dashes of red pepper
Few dashes of black pepper
2 pheasants, cut up
Salt to taste
2 tablespoons flour
1 cup milk

Heat the oil in a Dutch oven and sauté the onion until tender. Add the bell pepper and cook for a few minutes. Add enough paprika to color the onion a deep red and cook, stirring, for 1 minute. Add the tomato, red pepper and black pepper. Add the pheasant pieces, enough water to cover, and salt. Bring to a boil and reduce the heat. Cover and simmer until the pheasant is tender, about 2 hours.

Combine the flour with the milk and add to the pan, along with seasonings to taste. Cook until thickened, but do not boil. Serve over noodles.

*Since this is really a winter dish, you may prefer to use canned tomatoes rather than fresh ones, which seem to have no flavor in December. Since everyone has to work around the bones, serve this for family night dinner with homemade bread and green salad.*

"You take a big cock pheasant . . . He is not so much dinner as trophy, but when he is cooked correctly, he is not so much trophy as dinner, if you see what I mean."
—Robert Ruark, *The Old Man and the Boy*

# PHEASANT WITH WILD RICE CASSEROLE

1/2 pound sliced fresh
    mushrooms, or 1 (4-ounce)
    can sliced mushrooms
Butter
1 onion, finely chopped
1 cup finely chopped
    fresh parsley
1/2 cup chopped celery
1 (10-ounce) can cream of
    mushroom soup

1/2 soup can milk
1 cup grated Cheddar cheese
2 cups cooked wild rice
2 pheasants, cut into pieces
All-purpose flour
Shortening for sautéing
Paprika

Cook the mushrooms in butter in a skillet for 5 minutes. Remove from the skillet. Sauté the onion, parsley and celery until the onion is tender and golden brown.

Combine the soup and milk in a saucepan and heat until smooth and blended, stirring constantly. Add the cheese and mix well. Add the wild rice, mushrooms, onion, parsley and celery. Pour into a greased casserole.

Preheat the oven to 325 degrees. Coat the pheasant with flour. Heat a little shortening in a large skillet and brown the pheasant.

Arrange the pheasant on the rice mixture. Sprinkle with paprika. Bake for 1 hour.

*Top the pheasant with slivered almonds, if you wish.*

WILD FARE &
WISE WORDS

# SMALL
# GAME

# SMALL GAME

The quest for upland small game, most notably rabbits and squirrels, has played a formative influence in shaping generations of sportsmen. There is something about beagles, boyhood, and cottontails bouncing across a snow-laden field that evokes memories of the timeless art of Norman Rockwell or A. B. Frost. Similarly, it is well worth remembering that until the twin conservation success stories underlying the comeback of the white-tailed deer and the wild turkey, squirrel hunting was the single most popular sport throughout most of the South.

During a boyhood that found me outdoors on every possible occasion, I saw precisely ten deer by the time I went off to college at the age of eighteen. I never witnessed a wild turkey. Yet hunting squirrels and cottontails was an important part of my daily existence, from the opening of the bushytail season in mid-October until the close of the season for both species at the end of February. With me, as with so many other American sportsmen over the generations, squirrel hunting helped cultivate the traits that serve so well no matter what one's quarry. These include stealth, patience, persistence, solid marksmanship, understanding of the habits and habitat of the animal, the ability to read sign, stalking techniques, and much more. In fact, there is probably no finer apprenticeship for becoming an all-around hunter than lots of hours spent dealing with the treetop tricksters.

As for rabbit hunting, when it comes to plain good times nothing can quite replace the hallelujah chorus of a pack of beagles hot on the trail. The sport lends itself to camaraderie, closeness with canine companions, plenty of exertion, provided you are willing to fight the briars in efforts to "jump" cottontails, and lots of action. Best of all, rabbits and squirrels offer absolutely wonderful table fare. When I was a boy, my family ate one or the other at least a couple of times a week during the cold months, and as I look at these recipes that follow I find myself harking back with longing to those halcyon days of youth, wishing I could just once more sit down to a meal of squirrel prepared by Mom.

123

# BAKED RABBIT

1 whole rabbit
Salt, pepper and garlic powder
  to taste
Several small onions
Several celery stalks
1 onion, sliced

Several carrots
Bay leaf
Butter
All-purpose flour
1 cup water

Preheat the oven to 350 degrees. Rub the rabbit with salt, pepper and garlic powder. Stuff the small onions and celery into the rabbit. Arrange the sliced onion, carrots and bay leaf in a baking dish. Rub the rabbit with butter and sprinkle with flour. Place in the baking dish. Pour the water into the baking dish. Cover and bake until tender, basting often. *Makes 2 servings.*

# FRIED RABBIT

1 (14-ounce) can chicken broth
1 whole wild rabbit, dressed and
  cut into pieces
1 cup buttermilk
1/2 to 1 cup vegetable oil

1 cup all-purpose flour
1 teaspoon salt
Pepper to taste
Cajun seasoning
1/2 cup whole milk

Bring the chicken broth to a boil in a large pan. Add the rabbit pieces and boil for a few minutes; drain. Combine the rabbit and buttermilk in a bowl.

Heat the oil in a skillet. Combine the flour, salt, pepper and Cajun seasoning on a plate or on waxed paper. Remove the rabbit from the buttermilk and coat with the flour. Fry in the hot oil until golden. Drain on paper towels.

Drain the oil from the skillet, leaving 3 tablespoons. Stir in 2 to 3 tablespoons of the flour mixture and cook until brown. Combine the milk with an equal amount of water and pour slowly into the skillet, stirring constantly. Cook until thick. Serve with the rabbit. *Makes 4 servings.*

# Rabbit Fricassee with Mushrooms

1 cup all-purpose flour
1 teaspoon salt
1 teaspoon freshly ground pepper
1 medium rabbit, quartered (1 1/2 to 2 pounds)
1/4 cup olive oil
2 garlic cloves, chopped
2 bay leaves
1 large onion, chopped
1 (8- to 12-ounce) can tomato sauce
1 cup chicken broth
1 pound fresh mushrooms (wild mushrooms, if available)

Preheat the oven to 350 degrees. Mix the flour, salt and pepper in a large bowl. Dip the pieces of rabbit into water and coat with the seasoned flour.

Heat 2 tablespoons of the olive oil in a large skillet over medium heat and fry the rabbit until brown. Heat the remaining 2 tablespoons oil and sauté the garlic, bay leaves and onion. Cook until the onion is soft and translucent. Add the tomato sauce, chicken broth and mushrooms. Heat to simmering.

Arrange the rabbit in a baking pan and top with the tomato sauce mixture. Cover the pan with foil and bake until the meat is very tender, 1 1/2 to 2 hours. *Makes 2 servings.*

"If it is the lot of you husbands to be Skinners and Scalers,
why not go the whole hog and cook your own game? And put
some poetry and imagination into it. If you don't
like the result, just cover it with gravy."
—Havilah Babcock, *The Best of Babcock*

# RABBIT TENDERLOIN SATAY

MARINADE
$^1/_4$ cup water
$^1/_4$ cup soy sauce
1 tablespoon grated fresh ginger
1 tablespoon brown sugar
1 tablespoon cumin
1 tablespoon chopped cilantro
1 garlic clove, chopped
1 teaspoon Thai chili sauce
6 ounces coconut milk
2 tablespoons vegetable oil

RABBIT
1 pound rabbit tenderloin
   (8 to 10 pieces)

PEANUT SAUCE
$^1/_4$ cup smooth peanut butter
Juice of $^1/_2$ lime
1 tablespoon brown sugar
2 ounces coconut milk
2 tablespoons roasted peanuts

For the marinade, combine the water, soy sauce, ginger, brown sugar, cumin, cilantro, garlic, chili sauce, coconut milk and oil in a nonreactive bowl and mix well. Marinate the rabbit tenderloin in the marinade in the refrigerator for several hours.

For the peanut sauce, combine the peanut butter, lime juice, brown sugar, coconut milk and roasted peanuts in a bowl and mix well.

Soak wooden or bamboo skewers for 15 to 30 minutes. Thread the tenderloin onto the skewers. Grill over hot coals for 4 to 5 minutes per side. Serve the satay with the peanut sauce. *Makes 4 servings.*

# RABBIT POT STICKERS

8 ounces rabbit meat
2 ounces ground pork
2 tablespoons chopped black
  mushrooms
2 tablespoons chopped
  bamboo shoots
1 egg
1 teaspoon salt

1 teaspoon rice wine
1/2 teaspoon sugar
1/2 teaspoon sesame oil
1 tablespoon cornstarch
1 package round pot sticker
  wrappers
1/2 cup water or broth

Coarsely mince the rabbit meat. Combine with the pork, mushrooms, bamboo shoots, egg, salt, wine, sugar, sesame oil and cornstarch in a large bowl and mix well. Chill for 1 hour. Spread filling over each wrapper and fold to create small purse-like dumplings. Fry in a lightly oiled skillet until bottoms are brown. Pour in the water, cover the skillet and steam until the water evaporates. Serve with soy sauce. *Makes about 30.*

"It was a happy drive we had home, with the winter sunlight
streaming softly through the quiet woods and the hale odors of the
wild, free forest coming fragrantly to us. But dearer to the heart of
my humble companion were certain imagined odors: those
which were wont to set his soul on fire when that cloudy mountain
known as his Liza prepared his evening meal of corn-bread,
fried rabbit and snowy, steaming rice."
—Archibald Rutledge, *An American Hunter*

# Squirrel Potpie

1 onion, coarsely chopped
1 celery stalk, coarsely chopped
1 large garlic clove, minced or pressed
4 cups beef broth
Freshly ground pepper
1 squirrel, cleaned
Pastry for a 2-crust pie
1 (12-ounce) can Mexican-style mixed vegetables
1 tablespoon cornstarch

Preheat the oven to 350 degrees. Combine the onion, celery, garlic, beef broth, pepper and squirrel in a large pot and bring to a boil; simmer until the meat is very tender and easily removed from the bones. Debone the meat and set aside.

Measure out 1 cup of the cooking liquid and reserve. Fit the bottom crust into a pie pan.

Combine the meat, vegetables, reserved broth and cornstarch in a large bowl and mix well. Spoon the mixture into the pie shell. Top with the second crust, press the edges to seal and cut several vents in the top for steam to escape. Bake until the crust is brown, about 1 hour. Serve hot with a green salad. *Makes 4 servings.*

"I never turned a hair when confronted by roast
coon or a mess of chitterlings or squirrel-head stew."
—Robert Ruark, *The Old Man's Boy Grows Older*

# BAKED SQUIRREL

1 or 2 squirrels, dressed
Cold water to cover

1 teaspoon baking soda
1 to 2 tablespoons butter

Cover the squirrel with cold water in a large saucepan. Add the baking soda and bring to a boil. Remove from heat and rinse the meat well under running water, rubbing to remove any baking soda. Return to the pan and cover with fresh water. Bring to a boil, reduce the heat and simmer until tender.

Preheat the oven to 350 degrees. Transfer the squirrel to a baking dish, dot with the butter and bake until brown and crusty.

*This flexible recipe can also be used for rabbit, and it works equally well in a pressure cooker (which is a great discovery for tenderizing). The broth makes delicious gravy.*

# BRAISED SQUIRREL

2 squirrels, cleaned
1/4 cup (1/2 stick) butter
1/2 cup (about) milk
1 teaspoon chopped onion

1 teaspoon honey
1 tablespoon all-purpose flour
1/2 teaspoon salt
1/2 teaspoon pepper

Preheat the oven to 300 degrees. Cut the squirrels into serving pieces. Sauté in hot butter in a skillet until brown. Arrange the pieces in a baking dish and pour milk over them to a depth of 1 inch. Add the onion and honey. Cover the dish and bake until tender, about 40 minutes. Remove the meat from the dish. Pour the cooking liquid into a saucepan and whisk in the flour, salt and pepper. Cook over low heat, stirring, until thickened. Serve with the squirrel. *Makes 2 to 4 servings.*

WILD FARE &
WISE WORDS

WILD FOODS
& MORE

# WILD FOODS & MORE
## WILD FRUITS, NUTS, AND BERRIES

Man has always been a hunter, but throughout most of human history it was gathering, not hunting, that provided the principal source of sustenance. With that in mind, it seems only fitting that we devote some space to a celebration of recipes for some of the incredibly varied bounty to be found in nature's lush garden. In this chapter, we look at wild fruits, mushrooms and other wild vegetables, plus a handful of wild game recipes and delightful side dishes that are simply "other."

Gathering nuts and berries can be a special family adventure, especially if kids are involved, and it also offers a connection to the not-too-distant past. In my boyhood, for example, just two generations ago, it was common practice for entire families in the North Carolina high country to venture out for "pickings" several times each year. The first came when wild strawberries ripened, and I've always loved what Izaak Walton wrote about these delectable red jewels of late spring: "Doubtless God could have made a better berry, but doubtless He never did." Dewberries, a ground-running cousin of the blackberry, came next, followed in close order by black-cap raspberries. Patches of the latter were always easy to find during the winter, thanks to their distinctive purple canes, and hunters often filed away such discoveries for return visits a few months later. Then came blackberries, so plentiful many considered them a nuisance, and finally blueberries.

As summer gave way to fall, "nutting" took the place of picking. The sad demise of the American chestnut greatly diminished the importance of nuts in the diet of folks living close to the land, but there remained chinquapins, hickory nuts, beechnuts, pecans, and that prince of the nut family, the black walnut.

Nor should wild fruits be forgotten. Persimmons, pawpaws, crab apples, fox grapes, muscadines, and more are there for the taking. Provided, of course, you beat the critters to "nature's candy." The recipes here will give you a variety of ways to bring the outdoors to dessert or provide decoration for a cathead biscuit, dripping with butter, sure to bring salvation to even the most righteous of waist watchers.

## WILD VEGETABLES

There was a time when wild vegetables were widely utilized, but such
is no longer the case. Yet for those who know of them, where to
find them, and how to use them, wild greens, mushrooms, and other
delicacies can add interesting and inviting variety to the outdoorsman's table.

In the North Carolina high country where I grew up, pokeweed was, to use the local
vernacular, "as common as pig tracks." It was one of the first plants to put out new
growth in the spring, and it was easily located thanks to the dry stalks remaining from the
previous year. Another sure sign of ever-returning spring came in the form of ramps.
Mild to the palate, this wild member of the leek family, especially when eaten raw in a salad
or just dressed with hot grease, has an after-effect that redefines halitosis. These were
but two of many wild vegetables that form a fond part of my food memories and still
bring me joy when I have the opportunity to eat them.

## OTHER WILD FOODS

Fool around with wild foods long enough, particularly if you have any sense of culinary
adventure, and you will eat some pretty unusual things. Folks in the Sahara region
of Africa make a virtue out of dire necessity when they face locust swarms by dining
on protein-rich roasted grasshoppers. On a personal basis I've eaten a lot of offbeat game,
along with some fish, that proved to be wonderful. Examples include rattlesnake, alligator,
groundhog, gar, armadillo, 'coon, and even the backstraps from a cougar. In the case
of the latter, I remembered once reading that mountain lion was a favorite food of the
hardy trappers of the early and mid-nineteenth century, and the white meat, much like
pork in appearance and texture, proved to be delicious.

Maybe my most memorable food epiphany in this regard came from adolescent experiences
in trapping. Muskrat pelts brought as much as $3 each in the late 1950s, and that was,
to use my grandfather's phrase, real "cash money." On top of that, I soon discovered
that old Aunt Mag, a wonderful black lady who lived down the road from us, would
pay a quarter each for the carcasses. I was walking in high cotton, making money hand
over fist, and actually having enough to buy the occasional whole box of shotgun shells
(as opposed to buying them individually, which was common at the time).

Aunt Mag always had something simmering on the old wood-burning stove
that did double duty in cooking and heating her tiny home, and since
I gave her fish in the summer in return for exclusive worm digging rights in her
chicken lot, I was always welcome.

One bitterly cold winter day, returning from a rabbit hunt, I stopped at her house to
give her a couple of cottontails, partly so I wouldn't have to dress them. When I opened the
door, a tantalizing aroma of meat greeted me, and in typical teenage fashion
I inquired: "Aunt Mag, what do you have cooking?"

"I've got me a stew on the back burner," was the reply. "Get a bowl off the shelf
and try it." The stew, full of carrots, potatoes, onions, and a rich, red meat swimming
in a savory ocean of brown gravy, was absolutely delicious. After two heaping bowls it
occurred to me that I didn't recognize the meat. When I inquired as to what I had been
eating, a wondrous grin split Aunt Mag's ancient, wrinkled face. It was the moment
she had been waiting for. "Why, boy, you be eatin' muskrat," was her reply.
Then she chuckled in great delight.

That experience sends a clear message: Don't cast aspersions on what you haven't
tried, and if you are willing to venture out toward new food horizons,
pleasant surprises await you. That's exactly what these "other wild meat" recipes
do: offer a variety of dishes that don't fit neatly into any of the other
more commonplace categories in the preceding chapters.

## SIDE DISHES

While the basic thrust of this cookbook involves a celebration of nature's
wild bounty, there's no denying that "domestic" dishes have their part in game or
fish feasts. Who could think of sitting down to a main dish of squirrel and gravy
without a side dish of either cathead biscuits or sweet potatoes baked in their jackets?

Accordingly, this concluding section of the cookbook offers an interesting range
of what we have simply chosen to call "Side Dishes." You should find them
welcome complements to your game and fish feasts.

# WILD BOAR ROAST WITH SPICY BARBECUE SAUCE

4 to 6 pounds wild boar
   butt roast
1 cup water
2 cups white vinegar
2 cups mustard
1 cup olive oil

3 tablespoons paprika
3 tablespoons red pepper flakes
1 tablespoon garlic salt
1 tablespoon coarsely ground or
   cracked black pepper

Combine the meat and water in a slow cooker. Combine the vinegar, mustard, oil, paprika, red pepper flakes, garlic salt and black pepper in a bowl and mix well. Pour 2 cups of the sauce over the meat. Cook on Low for 8 hours. Serve with the remaining sauce. *Makes 4 servings.*

# PIG IN A POT

Wild hog shoulder or small
   ham, trimmed of most fat
12 ounces new potatoes, coarsely
   chopped
1 large onion, coarsely chopped
1 (8-ounce) can sliced water
   chestnuts

3 tablespoons teriyaki sauce
1 teaspoon ginger
1 tablespoon lemon pepper or
   Cajun pepper
1 (10-ounce) can cream of
   mushroom soup

Combine the shoulder, potatoes, onion, water chestnuts, teriyaki sauce, ginger and lemon pepper in a slow cooker. Cover and cook on Low for about 2 hours. Add the soup and stir to blend. Cook until the meat falls easily from bone, about 1¹/2 hours, a bit longer for a 5-pound cut of meat. Serve with stuffing, noodles or rice. *Makes 4 servings.*

# Dragon Wings

Several pounds alligator ribs
Salt and pepper to taste
1 cup peanut oil

2 tablespoons red pepper flakes
1/2 cup soy sauce

Cut the slab of ribs into individual ribs. Season a pot of water with salt and pepper and simmer the ribs in it for 30 to 45 minutes. Drain and chill. Heat the oil in a skillet over medium heat. Add the red pepper flakes and cook, stirring, for 4 minutes. Add the ribs and soy sauce. Cook, turning several times, until the ribs are brown.

# Muskrat with Mushrooms

1/2 cup all-purpose flour
Salt and pepper to taste
1 muskrat, cut into
   serving pieces
2 tablespoons butter

1/4 cup olive oil
1 cup sliced onion
1 cup sliced fresh mushrooms
1 (10-ounce) can cream of
   mushroom soup

Combine the flour with salt and pepper. Dip the meat into the flour mixture. Heat the butter and 2 tablespoons of the olive oil in a Dutch oven and brown the meat. Remove from the pan, add the remaining oil and sauté the onion and mushrooms until tender. Stir in the soup and mix well. Heat to a simmer. Return the meat to the pan, cover, and simmer until tender.

*Be sure to remove all small scent kernels and glands, particularly those underneath the leg joints. Leaving them intact can impair the flavor of this dish.*

# RACCOON STEWED IN RED WINE

1/2 pound bacon

2 raccoons, cleaned, boned
and cut into 1-inch pieces

1/2 bottle red wine

1 tablespoon tomato paste

3 (10-ounce) cans beef
consommé

Generous pinch of
ground thyme

1 tablespoon sugar

4 garlic cloves, minced

3 bay leaves

1/2 teaspoon pepper

1/2 teaspoon kosher salt

4 tablespoons butter

1/2 cup all-purpose flour

2 (4-ounce) cans mushrooms

2 (10-ounce) jars pearl onions,
drained

Hot cooked rice

Fry the bacon in a skillet until crisp. Remove from the skillet and drain
on paper towels, leaving the grease in the skillet. Brown the raccoon meat
in the grease, turning to cook all sides. Drain the grease from the skillet
and pour in the wine. Cook, scraping up all the brown bits. Whisk in the
tomato paste and cook for 4 minutes. Transfer the mixture to a soup pot.
Crumble the bacon and add to the pot along with the beef consommé,
thyme, sugar, garlic, bay leaves, pepper and salt. Cover and simmer for
3 hours, adding water or consommé if the liquid level seems low. Combine
the butter and flour until well mixed. Form into a cylinder on waxed paper
and chill. Cut the cylinder into small pieces.

Drain several cups of the cooking liquid and combine with the butter
mixture in a large bowl, whisking until well mixed. Pour the mixture into
the pot and cook, stirring occasionally, for about 1 1/2 hours longer. Add
the mushrooms and onions and cook for 10 minutes. Taste and correct
seasoning. Serve over hot cooked rice.

# Pure and Simple Poke Sallet

2 pounds tender poke leaves

2 tablespoons salt

2 tablespoons white vinegar

2 slices bacon

Wash the poke leaves well. Combine the leaves and a quart of water in a large pot. Bring to a boil and cook for 5 to 7 minutes; drain.

Fry the bacon in a skillet until crisp, then crumble. Combine the greens, bacon, drippings, salt, vinegar and enough water to almost cover the greens in the pot. Boil until tender, about 10 to 15 minutes. Pour off the excess liquid, but save enough of this "pot likker" to enjoy with corn bread. *Makes 6 servings.*

*Poke grows in untended ground in the spring and is best gathered in the spring. When gathering poke leaves, choose those less than 6 inches in length. Two pounds of leaves is about the equivalent of a paper grocery sackful.*

# Old-Time Poke

1 pound poke leaves

4 slices bacon

Salt to taste

1 hard-boiled egg, chopped
(optional)

Chop the leaves and combine in a large pot with 1 to 2 quarts water. Boil for 5 minutes, then drain. Repeat twice more.

Fry the bacon in a skillet until crisp. Crumble and add to the greens, along with salt. Add a little water and simmer until tender. Serve garnished with a little chopped egg. *Makes 2 to 4 servings.*

*The poke leaves are best collected from one- to three-foot plants. Try to collect only the uppermost leaves. They can be cooked in a little boiling water, then drained and frozen for several months.*

# "Kilt" Ramps and Branch Lettuce

2 to 3 slices bacon
6 to 8 ramps

Tender branch lettuce
 (saxifrage leaves)

Fry the bacon in a skillet until crisp. Remove from the skillet. Cut the ramps into lengthwise slices and sauté in the bacon grease. Serve with branch lettuce, topped with crumbled bacon. *Makes 1 serving.*

*Ramps are a member of the leek family and grow widely in higher elevations up and down the Appalachian range. Though mild-tasting, they have a powerful and lingering effect on the breath.*

# Wilted Dandelion Salad

4 cups very young tender
 dandelion leaves, washed well
 and drained
1/4 cup chopped chives
5 slices bacon
1 tablespoon brown sugar

3 tablespoons vinegar
1 tablespoon water
1/4 teaspoon dry mustard
1/4 teaspoon salt
1/4 teaspoon pepper
1 hard-boiled egg, chopped

Pat the greens dry. Combine with the chives in a salad bowl. Fry the bacon in a skillet and drain on paper towels. Cool the bacon grease slightly, then add the brown sugar, vinegar, water, mustard, salt and pepper and mix well. Pour over the greens. Top with the crumbled bacon and chopped egg. Serve immediately. *Makes 4 to 6 servings.*

# Buttered Spring Greens

4 cups any wild spring greens
2 tablespoons butter or
   margarine
Salt and pepper to taste

Hard-boiled egg, bacon bits,
   green onions and/or vinegar
   for seasoning

Sauté the greens in melted butter in a skillet until tender. Top with egg, bacon, green onions and/or vinegar. *Makes 4 servings.*

# Watercress Salad with Parmesan Mustard Dressing

6 to 8 cups fresh watercress
$1/2$ cup good-quality mayonnaise
$1/4$ cup milk
$1/4$ cup freshly grated
   Parmesan cheese

2 tablespoons Dijonnaise cream
   mustard blend
2 tablespoons fresh lemon juice
$1/4$ teaspoon freshly
   ground pepper

Wash the watercress and remove the large stems. Whisk together the mayonnaise, milk, cheese, Dijonnaise, lemon juice and pepper in a small bowl. Toss the greens with the dressing. Serve immediately. *Makes 6 to 8 servings.*

*The dressing keeps in the refrigerator for about a week and is good on Caesar salad.*

# Kudzu Blossom Jelly

4 cups kudzu blossoms
4 cups boiling water
1 tablespoon lemon juice

1 (13/4-ounce) package
    powdered pectin
5 cups sugar

Wash the kudzu blossoms in cold water, then place them in a large bowl. Pour 4 cups boiling water over them and refrigerate at least 8 hours.

Pour the blossoms and liquid through a colander into a Dutch oven. Discard the blossoms. (The liquid will be gray, but don't worry.) Add the lemon juice and pectin to the liquid. Bring to a full rolling boil over high heat, stirring constantly. Stir in the sugar, return to a full boil, and boil, stirring constantly, for 1 minute. Remove from the heat and skim off the foam with a spoon.

Quickly pour the jelly into hot sterilized jars, leaving 1/2 inch of room at the top. Wipe the jar rims, then cover at once with sterilized lids and rings. Boil the jars in hot water for 5 minutes. Cool. *Makes 6 half-pints.*

# Sassafras Tea

6 dried sassafras roots, each
    about 3 inches long
2 to 3 quarts (8 to 12 cups)
    water

Sugar or other sweetener
    to taste

Wash the roots well and combine with the water in a saucepan. Bring to a boil and simmer for 5 minutes or until the tea is dark. Sweeten if desired and drink hot from mugs, or cool the tea and serve over ice in tall glasses. *Makes 2 to 3 quarts.*

*Sassafras roots can be used several times to make tea, increasing in flavor each time.*
*Dig sassafras roots when the sap is down.*

# BAKED BRIE WITH PINE NUTS

$^1/_3$ cup self-rising flour

1 cup packed brown sugar

$1^1/_2$ cups pine nuts

$^1/_3$ cup butter, melted

1 large or 4 small wheels of Brie

Preheat the oven to 375 degrees. Combine the flour, brown sugar and pine nuts in a bowl. Add the butter and mix well. If you're using a small round of Brie, divide the topping into fourths. Place a small round of Brie in a small round baking dish and cut a cross into the top with a small sharp knife. Cover with $^1/_4$ of the topping mixture. Repeat with the remaining Brie and topping (or freeze the extra topping for up to 6 months). Bake the Brie until the topping is golden brown. *Each small wheel of Brie makes 6 to 8 servings.*

# CLOVER HONEY MUFFINS

5 cups oats

5 cups oat bran

2 cups chopped pecans or
   walnuts

$^1/_2$ cup unsalted sunflower seeds

$^1/_2$ cup dates

4 tablespoons baking powder

8 bananas, mashed

2 cups clover honey

4 cups skim or evaporated
   skim milk

4 egg whites

9 ounces applesauce

Preheat the oven to 425 degrees. Grease 24 muffin cups. Combine the oats, bran, nuts, seeds, dates and baking powder in a large bowl. Combine the bananas, honey, milk, egg whites and applesauce in another bowl and mix well. Stir the wet ingredients into the dry ingredients. Spoon into the prepared muffin cups. Bake for 20 to 25 minutes. *Makes 24 muffins.*

*The muffins will keep in the refrigerator for 1 week, or much longer in the freezer.*
*Reheat frozen muffins by microwaving for 1 minute.*

# CHEESE GARLIC BISCUITS

2 cups buttermilk biscuit mix
2/3 cup skim milk
1/2 cup shredded
   Cheddar cheese

1/4 cup melted margarine
1/2 teaspoon garlic powder

Preheat the oven to 450 degrees. Combine the biscuit mix, milk and cheese in a large bowl, stirring with a wooden spoon until a soft dough forms. Beat for 30 seconds. Drop the dough by heaping tablespoonfuls onto ungreased baking sheets. Bake until golden brown, 8 to 10 minutes.

Combine the margarine and garlic powder and brush over the warm biscuits before removing from the baking sheet. *Makes 10 to 12 biscuits.*

# BEATEN BISCUITS

4 cups sifted
   all-purpose flour
1 teaspoon sugar

1 teaspoon salt
1/2 cup lard or shortening
1 cup milk

Combine the flour, sugar and salt in a large bowl and mix well. With a pastry blender or 2 knives (or in a food processor with a metal blade), cut in the lard until the mixture resembles coarse cornmeal. Stir in the milk to make a stiff dough.

Turn the dough onto a floured surface and knead for 3 minutes or until smooth. Beat the dough all over with a wooden mallet, turning occasionally and beating the reverse side. After 30 minutes, the dough should have a satiny appearance and small blisters should appear throughout.

Preheat the oven to 350 degrees. Roll the dough about 1/2 inch thick and cut with a 1-inch biscuit cutter. Prick the surface with a fork and bake until the biscuits are a delicate brown, about 30 minutes. *Makes 36 biscuits.*

# HUSH PUPPIES

1¹/₂ cups white cornmeal mix
1 cup self-rising flour
¹/₂ teaspoon seasoned garlic salt
¹/₂ cup chopped onion
1 (8-ounce) can
   cream-style corn
1 egg
1 cup milk

Combine the cornmeal mix, flour and garlic salt in a medium bowl and mix well. Beat the onion, corn, egg and milk in a bowl and add to the dry ingredients. Place the mixture in the freezer while you heat the oil to 375 degrees in a deep fryer. Drop teaspoons of the batter into the hot oil. Cook just a few at a time until golden, turning to cook all sides. *Makes about 30.*

*To keep the shape and size of the hush puppies consistent, use a small scoop with a release mechanism, such as an ice cream scoop, and keep it in ice water between batches.*

# FRIED GREEN TOMATOES

4 medium green tomatoes
2 eggs
¹/₂ cup milk
¹/₄ teaspoon salt
¹/₄ teaspoon pepper
2 cups self-rising flour
Olive oil

Cut the tomatoes into ¹/₄-inch slices. Combine the eggs, milk, salt and pepper in a small bowl and mix well. Pour the flour into a medium bowl.
  Heat about 1 inch of oil in a skillet or electric skillet. Dip 1 slice at a time into the milk mixture, shaking off excess. Coat with flour. It's best to coat just before frying. Fry until golden on both sides. *Makes 6 servings.*

*This can be served as a side dish or appetizer. The tomatoes are good alone or served with ranch or blue cheese dressing.*

# Campfire Tater Jubilee

1 baking potato per person
Carrots
Zucchini

Chopped bell peppers
Butter
Salt and pepper to taste

Place a large sheet of aluminum foil on a work surface and top with another sheet.

Cut the potatoes into 1-inch cubes. Slice the carrots and zucchini to the desired thickness. Chop the peppers into small pieces. Place all the vegetables in the center of the foil. Dot with butter and season with salt and pepper. Fold up the inner piece of foil to enclose the vegetables and seal. Fold up the outer foil and seal. Place the packet in a campfire or on the grill for about 20 minutes.

# Roasted Rosemary Potatoes

4 new red potatoes,
    washed and dried
4 small Yukon gold potatoes,
    washed and dried

Olive oil
Kosher or other coarse salt
Fresh rosemary

Preheat the oven to 350 degrees. Prick each potato with a fork. Coat the potatoes with olive oil and place on a roasting pan. Sprinkle with salt and fresh rosemary. Roast until a fork slides easily through the center of the potato, 45 to 60 minutes. *Makes 4 servings.*

# Chestnut Dressing

1/2 cup (1 stick) margarine
1 cup finely chopped celery
1 cup finely chopped onion
1 cup cooked chopped chestnuts
  or pecans

6 to 8 cups corn bread crumbs
  (homemade is best)
1 egg, beaten
2 cups (or more) chicken broth
Salt, pepper and sage to taste

Preheat the oven to 350 degrees. Melt the margarine in a skillet and sauté the celery, onion and chestnuts over low heat for 10 minutes, stirring often, as the mixture burns easily. Add to the corn bread crumbs in a bowl. Add the egg and 2 cups chicken broth. Mix well. The mixture should be very moist; add more liquid if needed. Season with salt, pepper and sage. Spoon the mixture into a greased baking dish and bake for 30 to 45 minutes or until golden brown.

*To prepare chestnuts, cut an X on the round side of each chestnut. Combine with water to cover in a saucepan and simmer until tender, about 45 minutes. Shell and peel while warm.*

# Pear and Hazelnut Salad

1 cup whole hazelnuts
4 to 6 cups mixed salad greens
2 large pears, coarsely
  chopped

3 to 4 tablespoons mild blue
  cheese
Mild Italian dressing or
  raspberry vinaigrette

Toast the hazelnuts in a large nonstick skillet over medium heat, stirring often, until light brown. Place them in a clean kitchen towel while still hot. Fold the towel over the nuts and rub to remove the skins. Then chop the nuts coarsely.

Arrange the lettuce on salad plates. Top with chopped pears, toasted hazelnuts and blue cheese. Drizzle with a mild Italian dressing or raspberry vinaigrette. *Makes 4 servings.*

# Tomato Salad

3 tomatoes, cut into
   bite-size pieces
3 hard-boiled eggs, chopped
1/4 cup mayonnaise

1 sleeve round butter crackers,
   crushed
1/4 cup sliced black olives
Salt and pepper to taste

Combine the tomatoes, eggs, crackers, mayonnaise, black olives, salt and pepper in a large bowl and mix well. Serve immediately for best texture.
*Makes 6 servings.*

# Mandarin Orange Salad

2 large heads romaine lettuce
1/2 cup toasted pine nuts
1 large cucumber

2 (15-ounce) cans mandarin
   oranges, drained
2 cups crumbled feta cheese
1 cup Greek or Italian dressing

Wash and dry the lettuce. Toast the pine nuts in a large skillet over medium heat, stirring constantly.

Cut the cucumber into halves lengthwise and then cut into slices. Tear the lettuce into a large salad bowl. Layer the cucumber, oranges and feta cheese. Sprinkle with the nuts. Toss with the dressing just before serving.
*Makes 10 servings.*

"Our Christmas hunt ended at 8 o'clock, when we
returned in triumph to the plantation house, to a breakfast of
hominy, cold wild turkey, corn bread, and coffee."
—Archibald Rutledge, *An American Hunter*

# Pecan Curried Fruit

1 (29-ounce) can sliced peaches
1 (15-ounce) can pineapple
  chunks
1 (16-ounce) can pear halves
1 (16-ounce) can apricot halves
1 (16-ounce) jar maraschino
  cherries

1/2 cup chopped pecans
1/3 cup butter, melted
3/4 cup packed light brown sugar
1 teaspoon to 1 tablespoon curry
  powder, or to taste

Preheat the oven to 325 degrees. Drain all fruits and arrange in a
9x13-inch baking dish. Sprinkle with the pecans. Combine the butter,
brown sugar and curry powder. Sprinkle over the fruit mixture. Bake
for 45 minutes to 1 hour. *Makes 8 to 10 servings.*

*This dish is delicious with quail and other game dishes.*

# Tomato Topper for Burgers

1 medium red onion, thinly
  sliced
2 tomatoes, sliced
2 tablespoons olive oil

2 teaspoons lemon juice
1 tablespoon chopped fresh
  basil, or 1 teaspoon dried
Salt and pepper to taste

Soak the onion in ice water for 10 to 15 minutes; drain well. Combine
with the tomatoes in a bowl. Combine the olive oil, lemon juice, basil, salt
and pepper in a bowl or bottle and mix well. Pour over the tomatoes and
onion. *Makes 4 servings.*

*This topper is excellent on venison burgers and beef and makes a nice, simple side dish.*

# CORN AND BLACK BEAN SALSA

3 ears of corn, husked
2 cups seeded diced fresh
   tomatoes
3 tablespoons chopped fresh
   parsley, or 1 tablespoon dried
2 tablespoons freshly squeezed
   lime juice
2 tablespoons extra-virgin
   olive oil
1 tablespoon minced fresh
   cilantro

$^1/_4$ teaspoon minced canned
   chipotle chile in adobo sauce
$^1/_4$ teaspoon adobo sauce
$^1/_4$ teaspoon salt
1 (16-ounce) can black beans,
   drained and rinsed
1 green onion, thinly sliced
1 garlic clove, minced

Boil or microwave the corn until cooked through. Cool and cut the kernels from the corn. Combine the kernels with the tomatoes, parsley, lime juice, olive oil, cilantro, chipotle chile in adobo sauce, adobo sauce, salt, beans, green onion and garlic in a large bowl and mix well. Cover and refrigerate for 30 minutes before serving.

# CRANBERRY SAUCE

$^1/_4$ to $^1/_2$ cup sugar
1 (12- to 16-ounce) bag
   cranberries
$^1/_4$ cup orange juice

2 oranges, peeled, seeded and
   cut into cubes
$^1/_2$ teaspoon grated orange zest

Place the sugar in a nonreactive pot and heat over low heat until it melts. Add the cranberries, orange juice and orange chunks. Simmer, stirring often, over low heat until sauce thickens, about 30 minutes. Stir in the orange zest and let the mixture cool. *Makes about 3 cups.*

# Tartar Sauce

1 cup mayonnaise
2 tablespoons Dijon mustard
2 tablespoons chopped sweet
   pickle, drained
1 tablespoon minced capers
1 tablespoon minced fresh chives
1 tablespoon minced fresh
   parsley
1 teaspoon freshly squeezed
   lemon juice
Several dashes of hot
   pepper sauce

Combine the mayonnaise, Dijon mustard, pickle, capers, chives, parsley, lemon juice and hot pepper sauce in a medium bowl and mix well. Cover and refrigerate until ready to serve. *Makes 1 1/2 cups.*

# Seafood Cocktail Sauce for a Crowd

64 ounces Heinz ketchup
1 (5-ounce) jar ground
   horseradish
1/4 cup Worcestershire sauce
1 cup hot red pepper sauce
2 cups cider vinegar

Combine the ketchup, horseradish, Worcestershire sauce, hot pepper sauce and vinegar in a very large bowl. *Makes enough for about 50 servings.*

# Raspberry Sauce

1 (15-ounce) can raspberries,
   drained
1/2 cup white wine vinegar
2 tablespoons olive oil
1 1/2 teaspoons cornstarch

Combine all ingredients in a saucepan. Bring to a boil and cook, stirring, for a few minutes. Strain through a sieve to remove seeds. *Makes 4 servings.*

*This is a great dipping sauce for game birds and venison.*

# FRESH APPLE CAKE

1 1/2 cups vegetable oil
2 cups sugar
3 eggs
3 cups all-purpose flour
1 1/2 teaspoons baking soda
1 teaspoon salt
1 teaspoon vanilla extract

1/2 teaspoon nutmeg
1/2 teaspoon cinnamon
1/2 teaspoon cloves
3 cups chopped apple, peel on
1/2 cup raisins
1/2 to 1 cup chopped nuts

Preheat the oven to 325 degrees. Combine the oil, sugar and eggs in a bowl and mix well. Add the flour, 1 cup at a time. Add the baking soda, salt, vanilla, nutmeg, cinnamon and cloves and mix well. Stir in the fruit and nuts; the batter will be thick. Spoon into an ungreased tube pan and bake until a knife inserted in the center comes out clean, about 1 1/2 to 2 hours. *Makes 16 servings.*

# EASY BLUEBERRY BUCKLE

4 cups fresh blueberries or
  huckleberries
1/2 cup maple syrup
1 teaspoon cinnamon
1/4 cup cornstarch

1 1/4 cups all-purpose flour
3/4 cup packed brown sugar
1/2 cup (1 stick) butter, softened
1/2 teaspoon almond extract

Preheat the oven to 375 degrees. Combine the blueberries, syrup, cinnamon and cornstarch in a bowl and mix well. Pour into a greased 9-inch square baking dish.

Combine the flour and brown sugar in a bowl. Cut in the butter and almond extract with a pastry blender (or combine the mixture in a food processor) until the mixture is crumbly. Bake until light brown and bubbly, 30 to 45 minutes. Serve warm with ice cream, whipped cream or milk. *Makes 6 servings.*

# BERRY CRISP

1 cup quick-cooking or
  old-fashioned oats
1 cup all-purpose flour
1 cup packed brown sugar

$1/4$ to $1/2$ cup chopped nuts
$1/2$ cup cold butter or margarine
3 cups fresh or frozen berries
$1/2$ cup white sugar, or to taste

Preheat the oven to 350 degrees. Mix the oats, flour and brown sugar. Add the nuts. Cut in the butter with a pastry blender or in a food processor. Place half the crumb mixture on the bottom of a greased 8-inch baking pan.

Combine the berries and white sugar and pour over the base. Top with the remaining crumb mixture. Bake for 30 to 45 minutes or until brown and bubbly. Serve warm with ice cream or whipped cream. *Makes 4 to 6 servings.*

# CHOCOLATE CAKE

1 cup (2 sticks) butter, softened
2 cups white sugar
1 cup firmly packed light
  brown sugar
6 eggs
$1/2$ cup unsweetened cocoa
  powder

$2^{1}/2$ cups self-rising flour
1 cup sour cream
2 teaspoons vanilla extract
$1^{1}/2$ cups confectioners' sugar
$1/4$ cup unsweetened
  cocoa powder
$1/2$ cup half-and-half

Preheat the oven to 325 degrees. Cream the butter, white sugar and brown sugar in a mixing bowl. Add the eggs 1 at a time, beating well after each addition. Combine $1/2$ cup cocoa with the flour in a bowl. Add to the butter mixture alternately with the sour cream, blending well. Stir in the vanilla. Pour into a greased and floured tube pan. Bake for 1 hour and 20 minutes or until the cake tests done. Let cool in the pan for 20 minutes. Remove from the pan to a cake plate. Poke holes in the top of the cake. Combine the confectioners' sugar, $1/4$ cup cocoa powder and half-and-half in a bowl and mix well. Pour the glaze over the cake. Serve warm with vanilla or cherry ice cream. *Makes 16 servings.*

# Muscadine Jam

5 cups muscadine purée
1 package pectin
6 cups sugar

Measure the purée into a large saucepan. Heat, gradually adding the pectin. Bring to a full boil over high heat, stirring constantly. Add the sugar and cook, stirring, until it dissolves. Return to a full boil and boil hard for 1 minute. Remove from heat and ladle into hot sterilized jars, leaving 1/2 inch headspace. Cover with hot sterile lids and rings. Place in boiling water for 10 minutes. Remove and cool. *Makes 8 to 9 half-pints.*

# Persimmon Pudding

2 cups persimmon pulp
2 cups packed brown sugar
1/4 cup butter, melted
1 teaspoon vanilla
1/2 cup light cream or milk

2 eggs, beaten
1 1/2 cups self-rising flour
1/2 teaspoon cinnamon
1/2 cup raisins or nuts

Preheat the oven to 350 degrees. Mix the persimmon pulp, brown sugar, butter, vanilla, cream, eggs, flour, cinnamon and raisins. Pour into a greased 9x13-inch baking dish and bake until golden brown and just beginning to pull away from the sides, 30 to 35 minutes. Remove from the oven and cool slightly. Cover and seal tightly with foil or plastic wrap. Cut into squares and serve with whipped topping. Add 1 tablespoon bourbon, if desired. *Makes 6 to 8 servings.*

*Ripe persimmons are pale orange and very soft with wrinkled skin. To prepare pulp, rinse the persimmons in cold water and press through a non-aluminum sieve to remove seeds and skin. Use the pulp or freeze for later.*

# Hickory Nut Pie

Pastry for a 9-inch 1-crust pie
1 1/2 cups shelled hickory nuts
1 tablespoon vanilla extract or
   2 tablespoons maple syrup

1 cup corn syrup
3/4 cup packed brown sugar
3 eggs, beaten

Preheat the oven to 375 degrees. Fit the pastry into a pan and refrigerate. Set aside 1 cup of the larger pieces of hickory nuts. Pour the remaining nuts into a bowl. Add the flavoring, corn syrup, brown sugar and eggs and mix until the sugar is dissolved. Spoon the filling into the pie pastry, letting it settle. Scatter the reserved hickory nuts evenly over the filling. Bake until the crust is light brown, about 10 minutes. Decrease the heat to 350 degrees and bake for 35 to 45 minutes or until the filling is set and the nuts are brown. Let cool before cutting. *Makes 6 servings.*

# Black Walnut Banana Bread

1/2 cup vegetable oil
1 cup sugar
2 eggs
2 cups mashed ripe bananas

2 cups all-purpose flour
1 teaspoon salt
1 teaspoon baking soda
1/2 cup chopped black walnuts

Preheat the oven to 350 degrees. Grease a loaf pan. Combine the oil, sugar, eggs and bananas and mix well. Add the flour, salt, baking soda and walnuts and mix until thoroughly blended. Spoon the mixture into the prepared pan. Bake for 1 hour. Use pecans if black walnuts are not available. *Makes 12 servings.*

# WALNUT CAKE

CAKE
- 1/2 cup (1 stick) butter, softened
- 1/2 cup shortening
- 2 cups sugar
- 5 eggs, separated
- 1 cup buttermilk
- 1 teaspoon baking soda
- 2 cups all-purpose flour
- 1 teaspoon vanilla extract
- 1 cup chopped walnuts
- 1 (3-ounce) can flaked coconut
- 1/2 teaspoon cream of tartar

CREAM CHEESE FROSTING
- 3/4 cup (1 1/2 sticks) butter, softened
- 11 ounces cream cheese, softened
- 6 3/4 cups confectioners' sugar
- 1 1/2 teaspoons vanilla extract

For the cake, preheat the oven to 350 degrees. Beat the butter, shortening and sugar with an electric mixer set at medium speed. Add the egg yolks 1 at a time, beating well after each addition.

Combine the buttermilk and baking soda, stirring until the baking soda dissolves. Add to the butter mixture alternately with the flour, beginning and ending with the flour. Stir in the vanilla, walnuts and coconut. Beat the egg whites with the cream of tartar until stiff. Fold the egg whites into the cake batter.

Pour the batter into 3 greased and floured 9-inch round cake pans. Bake for 22 to 25 minutes or until a wooden pick inserted in the center comes out clean. Cool in the pans for 10 minutes; remove and cool completely on wire racks.

For the frosting, beat the butter and cream cheese in a mixing bowl. Beat in the confectioners' sugar gradually. Beat in the vanilla. Spread the frosting over and between the cake layers. *Makes 12 to 16 servings.*

# WILD STRAWBERRY TRIFLE

1 (18.25-ounce) package
  yellow cake mix
1 quart wild strawberries
Sugar to taste
Grand Marnier or other
  orange liqueur

3 packages vanilla instant
  pudding mix
6 cups milk
2 (12-ounce) tubs whipped
  topping

Prepare the cake according to the package directions. Let cool, then crumble.

Reserve a few berries for garnish and combine the rest in a saucepan with sugar and a dash of Grand Marnier. Cook for 1 or 2 minutes, until the mixture is juicy.

Prepare the pudding with the milk according to the package directions.

Cover the bottom of a large bowl or trifle dish with a layer of crumbled cake. Top with a layer of strawberries and liquid. Spread a layer of pudding over the berries, then a layer of whipped topping. Repeat the layers twice more, ending with the whipped topping. Garnish with the reserved berries. *Makes 16 servings.*

*Try the trifle with other types of berries. Chocoholics should try it with chocolate cake or brownies, chocolate pudding and crushed toffee pieces.*

# WILD STRAWBERRY BUTTER

1 cup wild strawberries
1 cup butter, softened

1/2 cup confectioners' sugar
2 teaspoons lemon juice

Combine the strawberries, butter, confectioners' sugar and lemon juice in a food processor fitted with a metal blade. Process until the mixture reaches a finely blended texture. *Makes about 2 cups.*

# BLACKBERRY DUMPLINGS

### BERRIES
I quart blackberries
I cup sugar, or to taste
I cup water

### DUMPLINGS
I cup all-purpose flour
2 teaspoons baking powder
1/4 teaspoon salt
I tablespoon sugar
I cup milk

For the berries, combine the blackberries, sugar and water in a saucepan. Bring to a boil.

For the dumplings, combine the flour, baking powder, salt and sugar in a bowl, then stir in the milk. Drop the mixture by tablespoonfuls into the boiling berries. Cook until the dumplings are cooked through, about 15 minutes. Serve hot with cream. *Makes 6 to 8 servings.*

# HUCKLEBERRY NUT BREAD

3/4 cup sugar
1/2 teaspoon salt
1/4 cup butter, melted
I egg
2 cups all-purpose flour
2 teaspoons baking powder

1/2 teaspoon cinnamon
1/2 cup milk
I cup fresh or thawed
  huckleberries
1/2 cup chopped nuts
Cinnamon sugar to taste

Preheat the oven to 375 degrees. Grease a 9-inch loaf pan. Beat the sugar, salt and butter in a bowl. Add the egg and beat thoroughly. Sift the flour, baking powder and cinnamon together. Add to the butter mixture alternately with the milk. Fold the berries and nuts into the batter. Pour into the prepared pan and sprinkle lightly with cinnamon sugar. Bake until the loaf is golden and a tester inserted in the center comes out clean, about 45 minutes. Cool in the pan for 10 minutes, then remove and cool completely. *Makes 12 servings.*

# INDEX

**Venison, Roast**
Barbecue Roast, 57
Slow Cooker Roast with
Cranberries, 56
Smoked Venison Ham or
Roast, 56
Venison Osso Buco, 59
Venison Shoulder Roast
with Vegetables, 58
Venison Stew, 79

**Venison, Sausage**
Baked Venison Ziti, 89
Glazed Venison Sausage, 81
Stewed Potatoes and
Sausage, 81
Venison Sausage
Casserole, 80
Venison Spaghetti, 86

**Venison, Steak**
Broiled Venison Steaks
with Parsley Butter, 61
Fajita Salad with
Caramelized Onion, 68
Ginger Steak, 60
Loin Steaks with Apricot
Mustard Sauce, 66
London Broil, 69
Steaks with Crab, Shrimp
and Scallop Sauce, 63
Thai-Style Venison
Salad, 76
Venison Loin Steak in
Brandy Cream Sauce, 61
Venison Steak Fingers
with Two Sauces, 77
Venison Steaks with Shrimp
and Asparagus Sauce, 62

Venison Steaks with
Shrimp Gravy over
Garlic Cheese Grits, 64
Venison with Lobster
Cream Sauce, 65

**Venison, Tenderloin**
Marinated Venison Loin, 57
Sweet Venison Kabobs, 70
Venison Loin Medallions, 67
Venison Wellington, 60

# THE WILDLIFE SHOP
P.O. Box 167 · Columbia, South Carolina 29202-0167
Phone 888-644-WILD (9453)

Please send _____ copies of *Wild Fare & Wise Words* at $19.95 each   $ _____

Shipping and handling; $6.95 for 1; $7.95 for 2; $8.95 for 3 or more   $ _____

TOTAL   $ _____

**Ship To:**
Name _____

Address _____

City _____ State _____ Zip _____ Telephone _____

**Credit Card Billing Address:**
Name _____

Address _____

City _____ State _____ Zip _____ Telephone _____

**Payment:** [  ] MasterCard   [  ] VISA   [  ] Check payable to The Wildlife Shop

Account Number _____ Expiration Date _____

Cardholder Signature _____

Please photocopy this form.